OLE BOUMAN

REAL SPACE
IN QUICK TIMES

ARCHITECTURE AND DIGITIZATION

XIX Milan Triennale

NAi Publishers

CONTENTS

RealSpace in QuickTimes. RealTime in QuickSpace. How's Life in the Digital Age?

Time and space, drastically compressed by the computer, have become interchangeable. Time is compressed in that once everything has been reduced to 'bits' of information, it becomes simultaneously accessible. Space is compressed in that once everything has been reduced to 'bits' of information, it can be conveyed from A to B with the speed of light. As a result of digitization, everything is in the here and now. Before very long, the whole world will be on disk. Salvation is but a modem away.

REALSPACE
IN QUICKTIMES

INTRODUCTION

Introduction

The digitization process is often seen in terms of (information) technology. That is to say, one hears a lot of talk about the digital media, about computer hardware, about the modem, mobile phone, dictaphone, remote control, buzzer, data glove and the cable or satellite links in between. Besides, our heads are spinning from the progress made in the field of software, in which multimedia applications, with their integration of text, image and sound, especially attract our attention. But digitization is not just a question of technology, it also involves a cultural reorganization. The question is not just what the cultural implications of digitization will be, but also why our culture should give rise to digitization in the first place. Culture is not simply a function of technology; the reverse is surely also true.

Anyone who thinks about cultural implications, is interested in the effects of the computer. And indeed, those effects are overwhelming, providing enough material for endless speculation. The digital paradigm will entail a new image of humankind and a further dilution of the notion of social perfectibility; it will create new notions of time and space, a new concept of cause and effect and of hierarchy, a different sort of public sphere, a new view of matter, and so on. In the process it will indubitably alter our environment. Offices, shopping centres, dockyards, schools, hospitals, prisons, cultural institutions, even the private domain of the home: all the familiar design types will be up for review. Fascinated, we watch how the new wave accelerates the process of social change. The most popular sport nowadays is 'surfing' - because everyone is keen to display their grasp of dirty realism.

But there is another way of looking at it: under what sort of circumstances is the process of digitization actually taking place? What conditions do we provide that enable technology to exert the influence it does? This is a perspective that leaves room for individual and collective responsibility. Technology is not some inevitable process sweeping history along in a dynamics of its own. Rather, it is the result of choices we ourselves make and these choices can be debated in a way that is rarely done at present: digitization thanks to or in spite of human culture, that is the question.

In addition to the distinction between culture as the cause or the effect of digitization, there are a number of other distinctions that are accentuated by the computer. The best known and most widely reported is the generation gap. It is certainly stretching things a bit to write off everybody over the age of 35, as sometimes happens, but there is no getting around the fact that for a large group of people digitization simply does not exist. Anyone who has been in the bit business for a few years can't help noticing that mum and dad are living in a different place altogether. (But they, at least, still have a sense of place!)

In addition to this, it is gradually becoming clear that the age-old distinction between market and individual interests are still relevant in the digital era. On the one hand, the advance of cybernetics is determined by the laws of the marketplace which this capital-intensive industry must satisfy. Increased efficiency, labour productivity and cost-effectiveness play a leading role. The consumer market is chiefly interested in what is 'marketable': info- and edutainment. On the other hand, an increasing number of people are not prepared to wait for what the market has to offer them. They set to work on their own, appropriate networks and software programs, create their own domains in cyberspace, domains that are free from the principle whereby the computer simply reproduces the old world, only faster and better. Here it is possible to create a different world, one that has never existed before. One, in which the Other finds a place. The computer works out a new paradigm for these creative spirits.

In all these distinctions, architecture plays a key role. Owing to its many-sidedness, it excludes nothing and no one in advance. It is faced with the prospect of historic changes yet it has also created the preconditions for a digital culture. It is geared to the future, but has had plenty of experience with eternity. Owing to its status as the most expensive of arts, it is bound hand and foot to the laws of the marketplace. Yet it retains its capacity to provide scope for creativity and innovation, a margin of action that is free from standardization and regulation. The aim of RealSpace in QuickTimes is to show that the discipline of designing buildings, cities and landscapes is not only an exemplary illustration of the digital era but that it also provides scope for both collective and individual activity. It is not just architecture's charter that has been changed by the computer, but also its mandate.

RealSpace in QuickTimes consists of an exhibition and an essay.

The exhibition was conceived as the Dutch entry in the Milan Triennial and consists of an installation designed by the architect Ben van Berkel, together with a large number of moving images demonstrating the digitization of our life world. The installation is explained in the first part of this book; a timetable is included at the back of it.

After a general introduction to the digital era, the four-part essay deals with three important ways in which the digitization process is influencing the world around us: Computer Aided Design, Smart Environments and Virtual Reality.

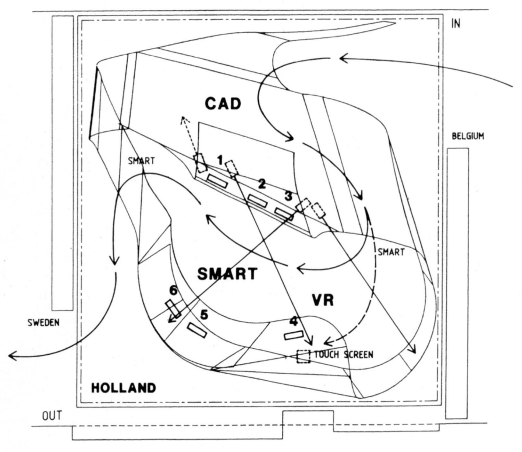

Pavilion, lay-out

The RealSpace in QuickTimes pavilion acts as a sculptural framework for an exhibition of multiple moving images. It provides a space that corresponds, within the given technical, organizational and financial limits, to the promises of electrotecture. At the same time it is intended as a documentary: in a series of films it shows us what effect the rise of the computer is having on the world around us.

REALSPACE IN QUICKTIMES

ARCHITECTURE

AND DIGITIZATION

THE EXHIBITION

The pavilion is not only about new digital spaces, it is itself a space, and the

public's experience of this space is of prime importance. To underscore this point, the pavilion contains a promenade architecturale. Starting out as a physical experience, at a certain point it switches to virtual mode where further progress involves mouse clicking or mindzapping. This is no mere entertainment; it is also intended to provoke critical reflection on the quality of the lifeworld in a digital age. The exhibition is actually a series of questions - posed in 3D and 4D - about the cultural reasons and spatial implications of the digital revolution. Major issues are involved:

- What standard of quality do we expect of life in the two-dimensional on-screen world?
- Who will get to experience this world, an elite or everybody?
- Will the user, whether from the elite or the masses, be understood according to the humanist view of mankind or according to some totally new view?
- Is life in virtual reality a case of life after virtue?
- If so, how are we to reclaim a morality?
- Can architecture sustain its role as a cultural metaphor?
- What will be the relationship between man and space in the new digital paradigm?
- What are the likely consequences of extensive digitization for the future of architecture as a material order?
- Can virtual space achieve greater richness than is presently the case, so that digital space can rightly be termed architectural?
- Should architects get involved with designing cyberspace?
- If so, will they wait until human experience of that world has become more dynamic, vigorous, inviting and profitable than in the real world, or will the changeover itself become part of their task? Should they lead the way?
- How will architecture evolve as an art, as a craft, as a discipline, as a profession, as part of visual culture, as a public sphere, as a cultural metaphor, or as a background to daily experience?
- How much of their former status will architects retain in the digital era, especially in view of their marginalization in the traditional building process?
- Will the boundaries of the familiar disciplines become blurred?
- If so, what effect will this have on the institutional relevance of these disciplines?
- What does the introduction of the computer mean for the role of the architect and for typological traditions?
- What are the margins for innovation and creativity in an art whose costliness and investment value is tied up with the constraints of the marketplace?

These are all questions that must be addressed by anyone interested in the destiny of architecture.

However:

It seems as if serious reflection on cultural and economical conditions has no place in the present debate on the rise and proliferation of telematics and multimedia. Anyone wanting to keep up with the state of the art seems to be condemned to abandon a critical stance vis à vis technological innovation and its organizational consequences. On the other hand many people in the field of architecture reject these innovations and have not the slightest desire to surf the latest wave of modernity. Another emerging division is that between the market-driven applications of computer technology and their user-driven appropriation by a few creative individuals who are able to adjust the available technology to suit their own agendas, if need be in collaboration with mainstream industries.

The exhibition is based on a belief that architecture has a key role to bridge   **The exhibition**

these gaps. It aims to show how the discipline of architecture, material in its conception but virtual in its potential, can feed the debate with ethical, economic and professional notions. To achieve this, it has brought together several participants in the regular building process in a non-profit situation.

The pavilion consists of three sections:

1) Computer Aided Design (CAD)

Nowadays, nearly all architectural offices are making use of computer technology and most architects are familiar with Computer Aided Design (CAD). This level concerns the design and construction of 'real' architecture using new technologies.

2) Smart-Tech

There is a lot of research currently being done into the use of smart tools and 'Domotics' in buildings; typical pilot projects are centred around eco-tech, climatological systems, surveillance techniques and telematic links. This level concerns the experience of 'real' architecture via new technologies.

3) Virtual Reality (VR)

Today a new spatial universe is emerging: Virtual Reality. Many people have already experienced completely simulated worlds. Meanwhile, Virtual Reality installations are becoming increasingly sophisticated. This level concerns the production and experience of virtual architecture using new technologies.

The architect of the pavilion is Ben van Berkel, one of the leading Dutch exponents of digitized space. He has produced a number of impressive projects using computer technology in recent years:

'To me, the computer is a way of radically breaking with the traditional design processes. The mediation techniques enabled by the computer signify a complete overthrow of many architectural assumptions, from the typology of organizational structures, to the hierarchical order of planning a structure, ending with the details. The computer entails a radical rethinking of the valuations implicit in architectural design. In this sense computational techniques could represent the first important development in architecture since modernism.'

Van Berkel's work is especially relevant to the study of computer software as a design tool. But his interest in the field goes beyond the mere rationalization of the design process and the delivery of flashy presentations; his prime concern is the way computational techniques are transforming and enriching the very nature of architecture. In addition, he is known as an exhibition designer, interior designer and civil engineer. As such, he was eager to embark on a project such as this which combines the reality of making material things with the virtuality of a world to come.

Van Berkel's design hosts a 'technological narrative'[1] composed of numerous video demos and on-screen computer artworks. These serve to demonstrate the state of the art of digital technology in the area of spatial and environmental issues, mostly in The Netherlands. CAD, Smart-Tech and VR are the main areas explored here and each is divided into two distinct levels: 1) commercial computer applications **The exhibition** being developed in a market-driven context; 2) the non-commercial individual search for new applications, new tools and new programmes, with the emphasis on the user-driven appropriation of computer potential.

[1] René van Raalte, partner in BRS Premsela Vonk, designers and architects, is responsible for the art direction.

Still from film in pavilion about market-driven and user-driven VR

Market-driven and user-driven Virtual Reality

BRTN

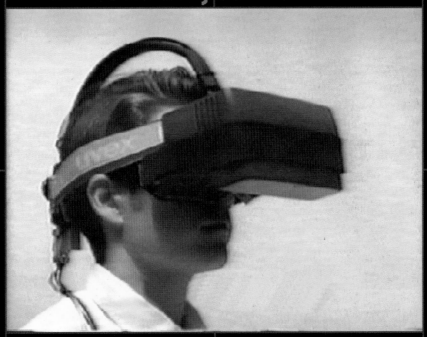

From the philosopher's stone

to

the philosopher is stoned

Market-driven
Computer Aided
Design

Delft University
of Technology
SIMONA

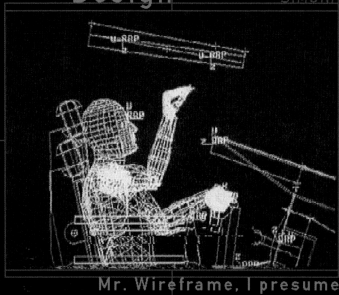

Mr. Wireframe, I presume

User-driven
Computer Aided
Design

Jan van de Pavert
House

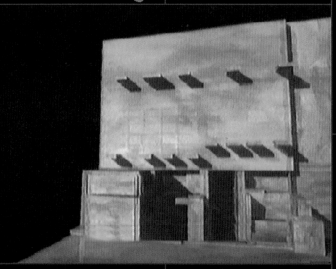

imitation or invention

Market-driven Smart-tech

IE
Keyprocesso

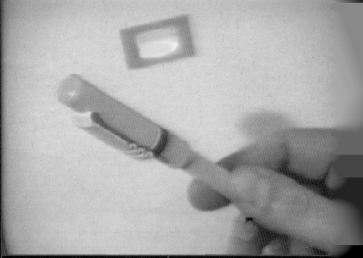

How's life in a trouble-free zone?

Jeffrey Shaw
Royal Roac
ZKM, Karlsruhe

User-driven Smart-tech

they can in fac
place additional demands on them

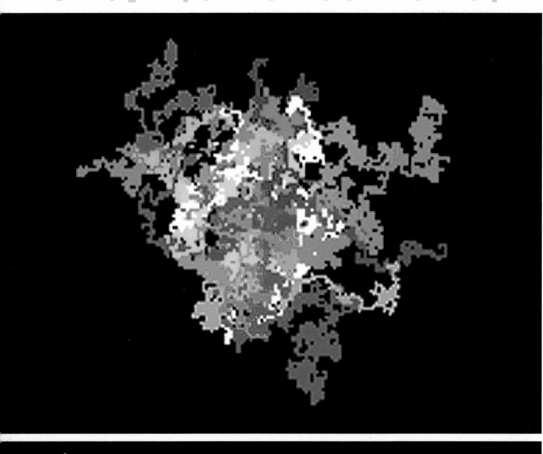

$$X_{i,t} = \sum_{j=1}^{t} e_{j_i}$$

Diffusion, Brownian motion

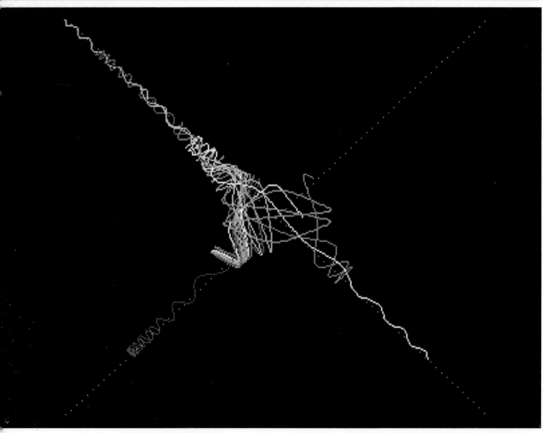

Magnetic quadrupole

Rossler attractor

$x' = -y - z$

$y' = x + ay$

$z' = b + z(x-h)$

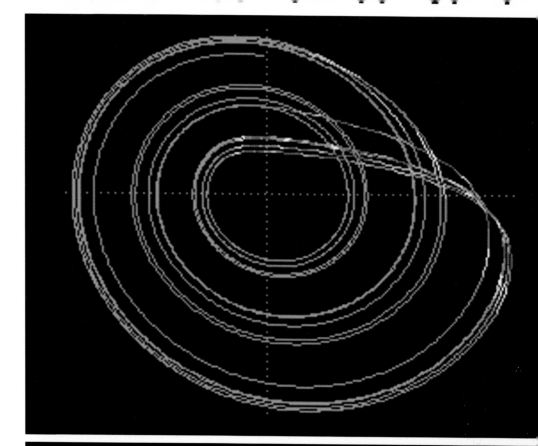

Three body problem

$V'_i = \$\,(M_i,M_j)\,d^{-2}$

Ben van Berkel, Yokohama Boat Terminal, 1994, artist's impression

NOX, exhibition pavilion on Neeltje Jans

Kas Oosterhuis, still from Sculpture City

WHY A VIRTUAL PAVILION?

The architecture of the pavilion represents the culmination of a series of projects developed by our practice in which computer technology has played an increasingly important role. The computer entails an entirely new approach to architecture because it challenges the automatic priority of the object; aspects of the tactile programme and aspects of the environment are directly intermixed. Since the computer does not discriminate among its input, all information is of equal value. As a consequence, internal influences and external forces are equally free to affect the materialization of a project. One of the most striking elements of the CAD design process is that information changes the output, which in turn alters the input, and so on and so forth; the essence of such transvaluation systems is that everything becomes unstable, floating or fluid. For us, this wave-like process constitutes the real significance of computational techniques - as the pavilion demonstrates.

HOW IS THE PAVILION STRUCTURED?

Structuring with the computer sheds new light on the concept of structure. The old idea of structure as the reproduction of a homogeneous, linear system has recently given way to a new view of structures which sees them as materializations in the process of becoming, based on shifting spatial techniques. Structures lose their specific, separate qualities and are defined more in terms of their relationship with the overall organization and their relationship to you, the audience/user: you zoom in on solid walls, you fluctuate along endless perspectives, space opens up on all sides; a multiplicity of mutations is possible, all unquantifiable, without order, without dimension, occurring as if in a fluid. It is this kind of structure that has shaped the pavilion. The limited nine-by-nine-metre exhibition space has been expanded with the aid of the amorphous, shell-like structure that suggests many different qualities. The structure is the exhibition's medium; it is a synthesis of digital and virtual space; it reflects projections and organizes the space.

PROJECT NOTES

Geometric model of the support, drawn in AutoCAD. The support is made up of planes and portions of cylinders and cones.

This drawing shows the model's geometrical construction in which the cylinder tangents have been used to achieve a fluid interface with the planes.

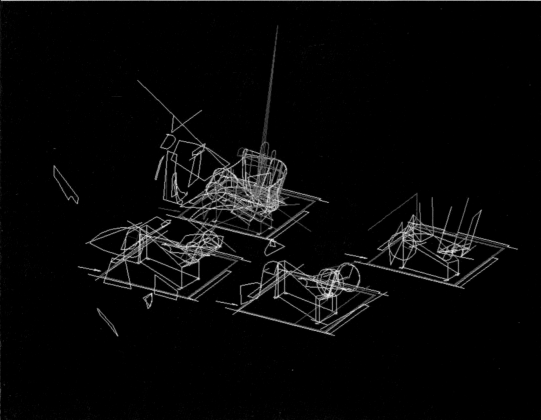

View of the wire model of the support. This drawing is part of the total geometrical model as shown in a and b, and was obtained by plotting most of the layers of which the model is composed. The renderings and the walkthrough were based on this wire model. The same wire model was used by the design engineers, Zonneveld Engineering, for their construction drawings.

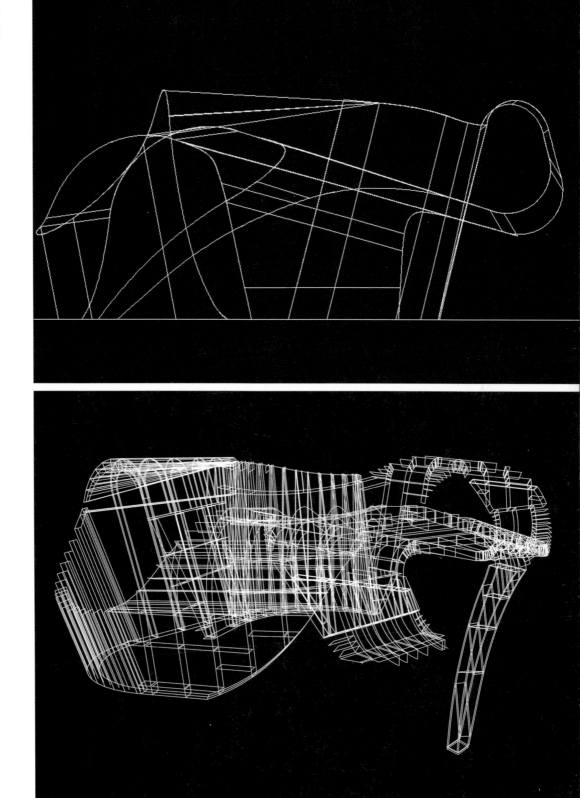

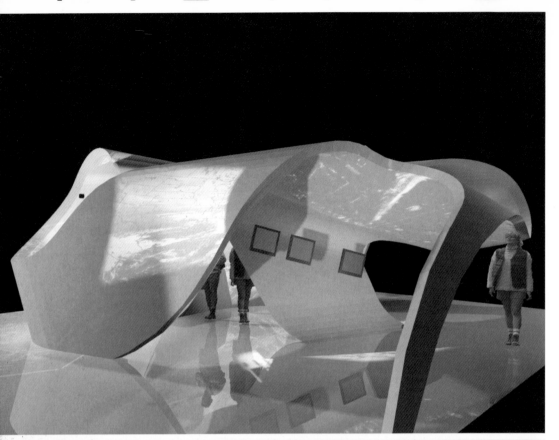

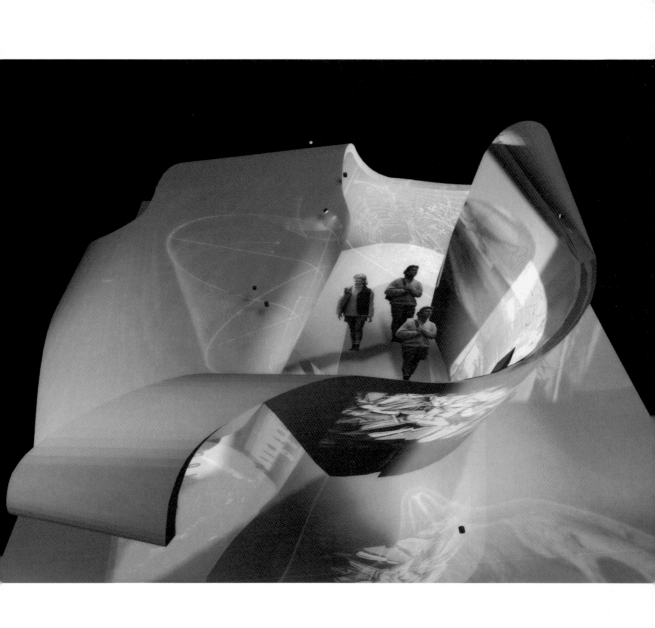

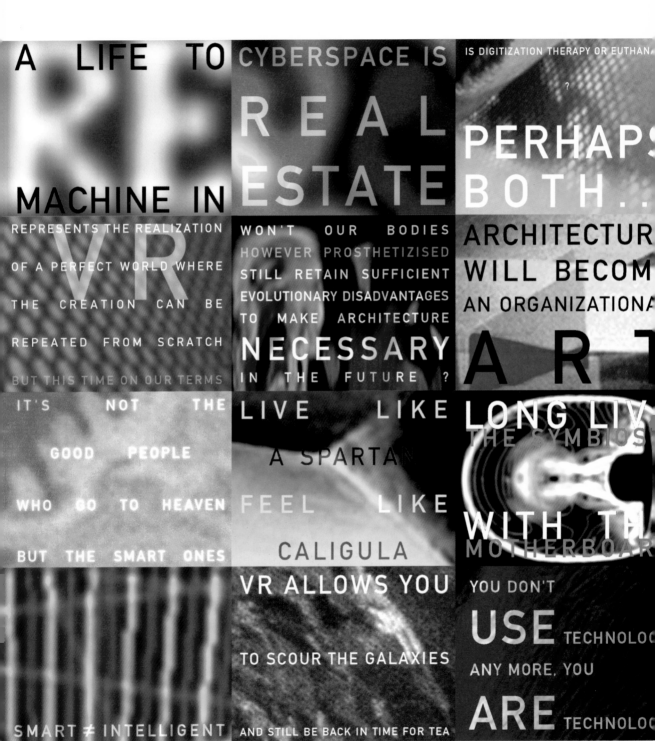

A LIFE TO

MACHINE IN

CYBERSPACE IS

REAL

ESTATE

IS DIGITIZATION THERAPY OR EUTHAN...

?

PERHAPS

BOTH...

REPRESENTS THE REALIZATION

OF A PERFECT WORLD WHERE

THE CREATION CAN BE

REPEATED FROM SCRATCH

BUT THIS TIME ON OUR TERMS

VR

WON'T OUR BODIES

HOWEVER PROSTHETIZISED

STILL RETAIN SUFFICIENT

EVOLUTIONARY DISADVANTAGES

TO MAKE ARCHITECTURE

NECESSARY

IN THE FUTURE ?

ARCHITECTUR...

WILL BECOM...

AN ORGANIZATIONA...

A R T

IT'S NOT THE

GOOD PEOPLE

WHO GO TO HEAVEN

BUT THE SMART ONES

LIVE LIKE

A SPARTAN

FEEL LIKE

CALIGULA

VR ALLOWS YOU

LONG LIV...

THE SYMBIOS...

WITH TH...

MOTHERBOAR...

YOU DON'T

USE TECHNOLO...

ANY MORE, YOU

ARE TECHNOLO...

SMART ≠ INTELLIGENT

AND STILL BE BACK IN TIME FOR TEA

EXIT

CYBERSPACE

ONDITION HUMAINE

CONSCIOUSNESS
INDUSTRY

NOW THAT'S A REAL

O PAIN, NO GAIN
UT NOW NOTHING
HURTS
ANYMORE

IS LIFE IN A
VIRTUAL WORLD
A CASE OF LIFE
AFTER VIRTUE ?

RENDER
OR
URRENDER

SEEING
=
BELIEVING

N ARCHITECTURE GO

IGIT-ALL ?

CD-ROMIFICATION
OF THE PAST
IS THE
PAX CYBERNETICA
OF THE FUTURE

The thing about paradigm shifts is that they can only be identified as such in retrospect. Only when the storm has died down is it possible to say whether the introduction of new technologies, changes in the conditions under which people work and the readjustment of existing ways of thinking, has led to a genuine change in the prevailing world view. So whether the digitization of architecture will in fact lead to new views as to what constitutes architecture, remains to be seen.

At the same time, the introduction of digital design technologies, the manipulation of experience by architecture-integrated (micro)electronics integrated in the architecture and the simulation of spatial experiences in virtual reality installations, are attended already by the unabashed celebration of a cultural revolution of unprecedented magnitude that is set to take place 'in the near future'. Going about our day-to-day lives we would still be recognized by our classical forefathers, but in our heads we have long been living in Cyberia. What are the options in our reaction to the multimedia revolution. Is it the après nous le déluge attitude? Is it the bonfire of the cybernauts? Or is there something else?

REALSPACE IN QUICKTIMES
CAN ARCHITECTURE GO DIGIT-ALL ?

THE ESSAY

THE BANISHMENT
TO CYBERIA

(IN WHICH THE QUESTION IS RAISED AS TO WHETHER ARCHITECTURE HAS ANYTHING TO DO WITH THE ELECTRONIC REVOLUTION AND IF NOT, WHY IT DOES AFTER ALL?)

It is two minutes to twelve. The media wind is rustling through the universe. And the jargonaut proclaims: 'The datasphere, the net, the web, electrotecture, netizens in simcity, the plug-in society, datarchitecture, the Orgasmatron, the electromatrix, the virtual grid, the morphogenetic resonance, the last paradigm, are all dimensions of Cyberia'.

Cyberia? It is the all-embracing term for the cyberspace of the Internet, of the multi-user groups in their MOOs and MUDs. And also for cyberspace as a metaphor for a new urban concept, full of neuromancing cyberpunks. And, finally, for cyberspace as hypertext, as the world where everything, literally everything, has become compatible. A cosmos like that in a disturbing dream where every new train of thought opens up a whole new reality. The universe as the one great cross-reference program from the almighty DataBoss. You don't hear much about it nowadays but cyberspace - now that's a real consciousness industry.

CHANGE

It's an industry where everything seems possible 'in the near future': perfect state control, total noncompliance, a democratic renaissance, even at long last an anarchist utopia. Both Brave New World and 1984. Ancient Athens and the virtual Gemeinschaft.

I shall certainly live to see that 'near future'. I don't know about you, but statistically speaking I'm good for another fifty years. And that's just in terms of current life expectancy. Given the developments in the treatment of Alzheimers, the manipulation of the gene for ageing, cryobiology and the conversion of our brains into the wetware of nervechips, I'm very much afraid that I'm likely to be active for a good deal longer. Active doing what? However happy I would be to retain until my dying day the oil paint on canvas, pencils on the drawing table and a Rotring on tracing paper, I am unable to ignore the daily evidence for the impending abolition of everything that has made what I did a hands-on activity. Even if I do not tangle with the world, the world will tangle with me.

certainly if the rate of change is governed by the same exponent - I shall most probably not even understand what I am

saying now. I shall have forgotten that I am (was). What's more, the moment my brain is connected to the Network, I

shan't know anything any more. That is to say, I shall know only how to find out that which I do not know.

But right now I'm old enough to be able to remember how it was and young enough to experience how it will be. I'm over

thirty - the age, so it's said, when personality is about to be stabilized. And now everything's up for review. Retirement

is still too far away for shrugging it off. Youth too long ago for a career as whiz-kid. No wonder that people turn

conservative at an increasingly early age. For while there is no guarantee that the world will get any better for the users

of the new technologies, it will certainly get worse for those who do not.

My home was my castle. Now it is oleb@xs4all.nl. Or is that my name? My identity, address and cyberhome are

theoretically exchangeable. There is nothing inevitable about my Net persona; it is dependent not on biology, birth and

social circumstances but on a readily manipulated, intangible product. Though born without a brass farthing, you can be

worth a gold sovereign on the net. Too bad that gold is also no longer what it used to be.

MODERN   WORSHIP

Cyberspace undeniably has immense cultural implications and is destined to have even greater ones. But at the same

time it lands us in a world where studying 'cultural implications' has become a hobby of the same order as 'arts and

crafts'. For the time being, however, I will venture the modest opinion that all the basic philosophical questions,

insofar as they are still asked, will be answered differently.

The burning issues addressed by Aristotle, Montaigne, Kant and Popper are no longer 'burning'. It's just Nietzsche

who survives. No sooner have we taken on board the collapse of the moral illusion than we are ready for the ultimate

epistemological one. Now that it no longer matters, we can think anything we like. Just when post-modernism has

created a moral vacuum, we can sign up for a crash course in information technology in preparation for logging on

to cyberspace. Devoid of any ethical basis, this is the culture of incessant 'keeping up with the latest developments'.

Catching up, day in, day out. No matter who you listen to in this bit business, they talk about an inexorable wave

that is rolling over us. And, as always, this inexorable event is presented as emancipation. The ascendancy of the

fast processor will finally free us from ourselves. It is emancipation into a state where we can abolish ourselves. In

the past we always demanded to see before believing. But now seeing = believing. The Enlightenment project has

lost the element of time. You are either Enlightened; or not. The ambition to bring more and more facts to light has

ended up by giving us a new piety.

Like every mature religious community, today's Modern Worship also has both its monastic and its mendicant

brothers. The monastics sit in huge research centres and launch one update after the other upgrade. The mendicants

are participants in the global lecture circuit. Because people all around the world feel that there is something

uncanny about life in dead hardware and dead software in living organisms, it's a circuit that is welcome

everywhere.

WIN   DOW   JONES

The rise of cyberspace betokens a new phase of modernity which consists, as ever, of fact (modernization) and fiction

(modernism). The impetus is still the same (wanting to be better than God and the autonomy of technology), but the

consequences are new. It entails a metamorphosis of the cultural landscape. And you don't have to look out the window

Above all else, the 'virtualization' of America, the 'Mindstyle of a New Generation', is profitable. Cyberspace is Real Estate. The much-ventilated hope is that the masses will learn to work with technology developed by progressive, counter-cultural entrepreneurs, designers and hackers. Freedom and spiritual emancipation seem to be no more than a modem away. But in reality cable networks are being sold to or provided by commercial mega-consortia. It's not the law that works against the hackers, but capital, anxious to exploit their services. For the first time in history, the threat to society is worth real money.

Such a macro-economic analysis suggests problems that do not exist (in theory, that is). It assumes a confrontational view of history, where history is seen as a continual struggle between being allowed to forget and being obliged to remember. That struggle has now become redundant. History is no longer a succession of problematical events. We now know that it is just a sequence of things which we have turned into a problem. If we stop doing that: no problems anymore. Marx's good old theory of capitalism with its holy trinity of labour surplus value, innovation and expansion, is as - no, more - valid than ever. But so what? Validity and actuality are no longer causally related. History is above all that which is no longer relevant. This is the deeper meaning behind the notion of the end of history. As to what is relevant nowadays - take your pick. Given the scale of the collective computer memory available around the world, no historical fact need yet be deleted and everything is simultaneously accessible. CD-Romification of the past is a Pax Cybernetica.

ARCHITECTURE IN THE PAX CYBERNETICA

What will happen to architecture in this peaceful future? A coherent prediction is impossible. With the world reorganized into accumulations of data, themselves composed of bits, we are living more and more in a staccato rhythm of 0 and 1. This condition scarcely lends itself to discourse, which wholly befits the fragmentary nature of a digiculture. For internal coherence is the very thing this culture is undermining. It is hardly surprising, then, that current futurology is more taken with the chaos theory than with well-founded prognoses.

Anyway, as for architecture we can distinguish at least two lines of development. First, we can consider what the future holds for architecture as profession, and second, what it will mean for our environment and thus for architecture as backdrop to our lives.

The computerization of all occupations and disciplines cannot be without consequences for architecture. Design will be further digitized and the experience of architecture will be increasingly regulated by integrated electronic applications. Will these developments serve to advance architecture? Or perhaps prevent its decline, even abolition? Will they help architecture to survive in the multimedia frenzy, or will they only help us to visualize architecture's terminal illness? Or even just to put up a good show at its funeral? Is digitization therapy or euthanasia? Perhaps both...

Is the use of computer technology in the design of architectural objects and intelligent spaces just a way of selling off architecture as the carrier of imagination? Or does that technology facilitate a new sort of imagination? Is it a means to an architecture that helps people to lead more pleasant lives, or just a means of enabling architecture to survive as a separate discipline? The key question is whether we will acquire better, healthier, more inspiring and more beautiful environments by means of computers. Or is their role simply to produce and let us experience, buildings 'appropriate to our time'?

If we are going to spend more and more time in cyberspace the question will arise as to what extent the physical environment still matters. Is architecture still architecture once it has been transplanted to Amplified Intelligence? Is still architecture? As soon as our communications become part of a virtual network, only the promise of mobility and accessibility seems to offer an adequate metaphor. And that doesn't require much in the way of architecture as a physical reality.

The new reality that will be our lot 'in the near future', is beyond any metaphorical description of 'reality', and that spells the loss of architecture's age-old beriëe. But won't there perhaps be enough reality left over to justify architecture? Won't even the android want to retain something of the biological and phenomenological quality of architecture? In other words, won't our bodies, however prostheticized, still retain sufficient evolutionary disadvantages to make architecture necessary in the future, too?

Even if these questions are answered in the negative, there is still hope. If not for architecture, then certainly for architects. They can shift their field of endeavour to cyberspace itself. There is much work to be done there by way of augmenting the spatial richness. Nevertheless, a qualification is in order here. The 'space' in 'cyberspace' is a metaphor whose scope is as yet unknown. It is only very recently that architecture has claimed the concept of space for itself. So although many (modern) architects see themselves as specialists of space, this is in fact very relative when seen in the light of eternity. The assumption that cyberspace is an architectural issue is therefore open to question. Nonetheless, the metaphor prompts architects to think that cyberspace has something to do with them. Yet it might well be that talking about 'space' simply makes it easier to understand and to accept the abstraction of the datasphere. It wouldn't be the first time that a major innovation had been dressed up in old clothes.

Even so, this qualification does not get to the crux of the matter. Which is that our relationship with the material world is getting weaker by the day. Now that everything is reduced to information in a data program, even 'matter' can attain the 'speed of light' without becoming infinitely heavy. $E = mc^2$? That's all behind us.

And just as well, because if architecture were to stay as it is, that is to say, solid and static, it would contribute to an ecological disaster. (At the present moment, for instance, the building industry alone consumes more wood than is being replanted world-wide.) It couldn't go on like this forever. Architecture had to be tamed, and homo faber replaced by homo cyberludens, a game boy, a terminal identity who can at least remain seated in his chair, logged on to the Net. In this version of the future what remains of the physical environment is a 'trouble-free zone'. All the stress and anxiety that went with the tyranny of distance in time and space is alleviated by an endless quantity of intelligent products.

Is this all there will be? Perhaps there are other versions. When we ask ourselves what will be the mandate for architecture in the digital future, we can distinguish three different fields of action. 1) Computer Aided Design and its role in the conception of architecture. 2) The emergence of Intelligent Buildings and Smart Spaces. 3) The parallel universe of Virtual Reality. Each field is bound to the tension between market requirements and the private endeavors of some individuals, aspiring to raise the standard of our lifeworld. In the following chapters an effort is made to map each of these fields.

Charles Cockerell, The Professor's Dream, 1848

in **QuickTimes**

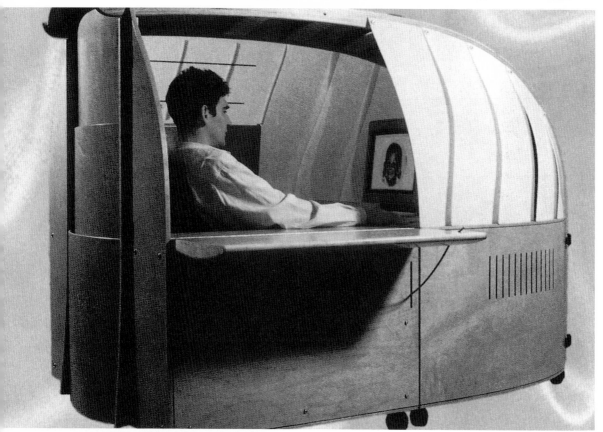

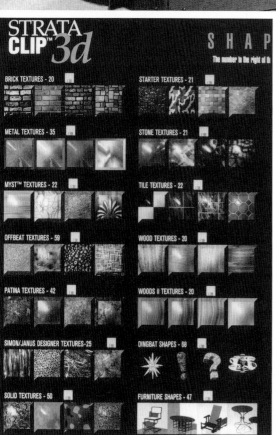

STRATA CLIP™ 3d

SHAP

The number to the right of th

BRICK TEXTURES - 20	STARTER TEXTURES - 21
METAL TEXTURES - 35	STONE TEXTURES - 21
MYST™ TEXTURES - 22	TILE TEXTURES - 22
OFFBEAT TEXTURES - 59	WOOD TEXTURES - 20
PATINA TEXTURES - 42	WOODS II TEXTURES - 20
SIMON/JANUS DESIGNER TEXTURES-25	DINGBAT SHAPES - 68
SOLID TEXTURES - 50	FURNITURE SHAPES - 47

RENDER OR SURRENDER

(IN WHICH THE QUESTION IS POSED: DOES CAD STAND FOR CONTROL-ALT-DELETE[1] VITRUVIUS OR WILL IT ACTUALLY DO ARCHITECTURE SOME GOOD?)

In this chapter I want to explore further the extent to which the trend towards immateriality is visible in everyday architectural practice, where solid buildings are still being turned out on the basis of solid programmes and solid figures, but where increasing use is being made of computer facilities. The question is this: what role does Computer Aided Design play as an element in the digitization of our culture?

Enter any ambitious architectural office nowadays and you can't help noticing that drawing tables are on the way out. Sketching boards have disappeared and pencils lie around unused. While specialist suppliers in drawing materials are going bankrupt architectural offices are switching en masse to the computer. Even though most of the current software imitates the old situation, the conditions under which the design is produced have changed irrevocably.

Ask why this is necessary and the standard answer is that it is faster, better, more elegant. Plus, of course, more efficient and hence cheaper. Just take a random look at what it can do: correct mistakes, calculate costs, test colours and textures without incurring expensive man-hours, compile a digital catalogue of building components, dazzle clients with trendy presentations from every conceivable viewpoint, assess designs in the light of building regulations, produce cross-sections - just ask and any halfway decent program will do it for you. What a saving and how easy. Clients fall over themselves...

[1] The play on words comes from Manfred Plotegg

DELIRIOUS CYBERIA

The introduction of computer aided drawing and designing can be seen as an important step in the much longer process of rationalization that already has innumerable professions in its grip. Although the building industry, by virtue of its internal organizational structure and the organic nature of capital, is a traditionally conservative sector where innovation tends to be sluggish and incidental, it cannot escape the latest wave of modernity issuing from power points, telephone lines and cable terminals. It's taken a while but now architecture, too, is plugged in to the electronic revolution.

This development also serves to reinforce the tendency to treat architecture as a spectacle. Considerable energy and intelligence is being thrown into improving the presentation of architecture. Architects are now eagerly exploiting the layman's inability to read architectural drawings by showing seductive animations which pander to the client's secret longing to count for something in this world. No matter how predictable and lifeless the actual design, making a videoclip of it seems to lend it visionary qualities.

Even architects fall for spectacle. No architect who has had any contact with the phantasmagorical images of aerodynamics, biotechnology or industrial design, who has experienced fractals or video drugs, can remain in awe of classic axonometrics or bird's-eye views. The seductive power of these images from unsuspected worlds turns the tradition of architectural representation on its head. The result is a total shake-up of the powers of perception, and dynamization of the drawing. What's more, this might just prove to be the path by which architecture can retain some kind of role in a fragmented building process. The imagination, virtually excluded from the materialization of the design, is now turning its attention to its representation. Delirious Cyberia.

Nevertheless, these are early days still. No matter how advanced the current software may seem, compared with the promises it makes we are still at the prehistoric stage. The promise is of a computer-generated architecture that is more than the sum of endless calculations; it is of an architectural guild which uses computer power to produce something unforeseen, which is not only intent on working faster and more economically but which also aspires to create great new wonders and which wants the profession to learn from itself. It is a matter of searching for an architecture that will either open up a vast new arena for individual expression - to the extent that it still exists - or allow room for chance, which exceeds all individual expression. In both cases what it comes down to is the exploring, even writing of new software that will fully exploit the hardware's potential. And this is the very area that is as yet largely unexplored.

STEERING THE USER ALONG WELL-WORN PATHS

Before going on to examine early efforts in this direction, first a brief sketch of mainstream Computer Aided Design (or Computer Aided Drafting). I am thinking here mainly of AutoCAD, a program used by a lot of offices and one which, insidiously and, given its one-sidedness, to the irritation of many, has developed into a standard of sorts. Linked to an architectural application and other extensions, AutoCAD is capable of taking care of drafting, calculation, presentation and management, in short a fair slice of the production cycle of a building. The standardized format in which drawings are stored allows for problem-free data exchange via the modem or an internal network, while a growing library of building components - compiled to one's own specifications, of course - speeds up the process of assembling a design. In the presentation phase there are any number of application programs that can be invoked to optimize the design's persuasiveness (read: visual realism). Computer renderings can now approximate photorealistic quality. On the other hand, although these renderings may impress, they do not necessarily lead to understanding. The presentation software currently available, despite all appearances to the contrary, is still unable to provide an integrated picture of the relationship between form, programme, materialization and costs. However easy, flexible and efficient most drawing program extensions may in many respects be, they inhibit creative computer use. For one thing, everything in the standard software is geared to solving notorious architectural problems. Because most architects see themselves as service providers, the makers of design software also think exclusively in terms of service. That is after all their market. What is lacking is a speculative level where architecture can be deployed to explore the strengths and paradoxes of a given program. Although the average architect will view the automatic solution of architectural problems as a happy release from a bad dream, for a creative mind it is more of an impediment than an improvement. For innovative architecture the presence of a catalogue of building components is nothing short of disastrous. The catalogue's very convenience turns it into a new tyranny. In architecture only the greatest can get away with doing it the hard way if there is an easier way of doing things. To be perfectly blunt: the software industry is not in the business of inventing things that don't pay.

Then again there is the conflict between 2D and 3D, which in practice leads to a strict separation between drafting and designing. In many design programs no correction is possible once a design has been turned into a 3D model. Programs that allow changes at the image synthesis stage are few and far between and in any case the necessary hardware is far too expensive for the average architectural firm. Which means, in effect, that there is precious little evidence of CAD's much-vaunted promise to integrate creativity and practical effect. So if you 'walk' through your building using the WalkThrough program or extension, and you don't like it, you have no option but to return to the CAD program in order to put things right. Not only does the architect remain imprisoned in abstractions, he is also robbed of his powers of imagination by an all too easy translation of these abstractions into slick images that permit no (real time) interactivity. Thus architecture is more than ever imprisoned in its own idiom, a much-reduced repertoire of pre-programmed shapes, functional elements and standard linkages. All in all, the greatest drawback of the average software package is that it asks only rhetorical questions. The menu bar steers the user along well-worn paths. What is missing is the element of surprise, the possibility of discovering new problems for architecture.

BUILDING BECOMES DATA MANIPULATION

Only when Computer Aided Design reaches the stage where communication between design partners, between different programs and between networks is fully 3D, will it be possible to start exploring Cyberia in a manner which, rather than reducing architecture to mere calculation, will usher in the next phase of its history. Instead of reductive abstractions it will be about generative abstractions which will help to make architecture elastic and liquid. The development of software, still in its infancy in architecture but already extensively employed in more capital-intensive sectors, will acquire a dynamics of its own, no longer derived from representational clichés. Imitation will become invention. Drawing, designing and representation in one and the same program! The inertia of architecture, from time immemorial both symbol of and obstacle to its progress, will be temporarily set aside during the design process. For once, flexibility and absence of scale are not the familiar slogans of an over-rationalized architectural practice, but the preconditions for reinventing architecture. And so we approach the seamless integration of interactive sketching, modelling, photo-realistic representation and forays into hyper-reality, all in the one application. The computer changes from a mere tool into an environment where the manipulation of factual data can be combined with a flight of fancy.

The computer, used in this way, makes possible a new architecture. Virtually all buildings are still conceived as a

reiteration of a known type. They look the way we expect them to look. A house looks like a house. Top is top and bottom is bottom; the architect shows enormous respect for tradition and usually thinks in

terms of object types. Loyalty towards materials, functions or structure is still the top priority. In other words, the introduction of the computer is in most cases no more than an efficiency drive within the framework of time-honoured procedures in equally traditional architectural firms. But a truly experimental use of the computer could change all that. And we are not talking about a revolution within a single firm but of the entire discipline. Building would become data manipulation, the making of system types rather than object types. The element of chance introduced into design as a result of complex algorithms, supersedes the reliance on the necessarily limited idiom of the individual designer. Strong form and elegant details lose their relevance. (According to Mies van der Rohe, God was in the details; but God was dead and Mies's details didn't know it yet.) The 'third skin' has become a network. The stage is set for non-intentional architecture. Instead of just thinking up shapes the architect can lay down the terms and the ground rules for data manipulation, leaving the user to 'finish off' the work. Since there is no longer any rule saying that one architecture is superior to another, and we are therefore saddled with a grotesque carnival of forms, we would be better off turning architecture into a materialized Rorschach test where it is the user who dictates the meaning. Who would have thought that 'binarity' would lead to the rebirth of the organic building. And to 'participatory building'. It is no longer necessary to refer back to image in the designer's head during the course of the design process. The design itself forms an image. Designing becomes a question of writing and correcting algorithms. The building as disciplining machine - encasing and framing our lives - may not disappear immediately, but the building that brandishes this function like an icon probably will. Some architects are already tentatively starting to think of architecture as a 'field'; to see buildings as a collection of flexibly integrated fields of influence, without being hampered by the old preoccupation with form and contour. Intrinsic beauty of form is a thing of the past. In the wake of Claude Perrault, who brushed aside the Vitruvian canon and reduced the classic orders to a matter of (subjective) personal choice, we now have, say, SOFTIMAGE. So long as you have the right software (for example Mathematica, FORM-Z, Alias/Wavefront products) and a hefty ration of innocence, working with the computer is entirely free of preconceptions. All variables are fusible in a process of hybridization, leading to new, undreamt of system typologies. This, surely, is the liquid architecture that will make me drunk.

HETEROTROPY

Drunk? What I mean is this: in talking about the digitization of the design process it is difficult to suppress a certain degree of excitement, particularly when one is anxious to avoid an all too easy scepticism. And once you lose yourself in the promise that the computer represents for the future of architecture you are, paradoxically enough, doomed to enthusiasm. No matter how concerned you are by the crisis in 'making' under a late-capitalist order, where even architecture is ultimately no longer a 'thing in the world' but a mere data packet; or by the way the 'scientific nature' of binary logic has been fetishized; or by the fact that small-scale design offices clearly lack the capital to be able to work with the hardware that is necessary for the above-mentioned modernization; or by the lack of expertise and programming know-how that would allow such under-capitalized offices to start writing their own software; or by a building industry that is so behind the times that it is scarcely aware of the possibilities available in, say, the car industry and which does little in the way of innovation; or by the fact that the entire computer, and hence also CAD, industry is rooted in the military's Cold War version of reality; or by the inability of most programmers to think in terms of iconography and their total fixation with spatial ornamentation - no matter how much of a burden all this places on the

future of creative computer usage, the fact is that an elementary criterion of architectural quality, the manipulation of the parallax effect, is set to undergo a revolution. This criterion, relegated to oblivion in post-modernism, is experiencing a rebirth. The freeing up of space brought about by industrial construction techniques was an enormous step forward in the history of architecture. With the help of the computer even construction may become irrelevant, or at the very least lose its moralizing significance. Then architecture will have survived the - apparently not so eternal - distinction between carrier and carried, support and load. The Modern space was isotropic, the cybernetic space will be heterotropic, that is to say free of any distinction between horizontal and vertical. What an experience awaits us!

FROM PARADISE.

For a long time now he had wanted to be dead, to go to heaven, to finally claim his share of eternal peace. Of course, he appreciated all those achievements of the consumer society, that great, unending enjoyment. It was wonderful that the end of dialectics was almost a fait accompli and that there was an excellent metamedia theory of representation with which to neutralize even the most distressing pictures from other parts of the world. Fine, too, that solidarity had been unmasked as an invention of materialist collectivism and the socialists and conservatives were able to join forces. All the same...

The jet lag that hit you on your way back from a subsidized orientation trip to Las Vegas or Orlando or Tokyo was as disagreeable as ever; you still felt like shit. And then there were all those irritating minor ailments that had still not been conquered: the coughs and colds, a hiccup in the immune system, you succumbed so easily. All in all, the ingredients of paradise might have been imported here on earth but ultimate perfection was still reserved for the kingdom of heaven. Surely it must offer something better than all this eternal zapping from one pleasure to another: a totally transparent interface between all kinds of orgasm.

His friends, to the extent that they still merited the name, were worried. So young and already tired of life. To have everything and still long for fulfilment, for apotheosis. So they devised a ruse.

Next day he awoke in a strange bedroom. He found himself lying in a four-poster bed, under a magnificent canopy. No trace of a pea under any of the pillows, his body just seemed to float, weightless, on the eiderdown. A cord hung from the canopy. He rang and presently a flunkey entered the room and enquired what sir desired. 'Salmon, toast and champagne.' In no time at all his order appeared on the bed-side table. While he tucked into this food for the gods, he was able to enjoy the sound of angels playing their harps and sirens singing songs such as no mortal had ever heard.

And there he continued to recline, constantly plied with superior wines and the choicest foods. He did not feel his body, he lacked for nothing. In the evening the flunkey returned with all that his heart could desire. He had only to think of something pleasant and immediately all that was fine and good was paraded before him. No sooner did he think of loved ones and friends than they were there with him, in him. In the end, everything around him was nothing more than the constant realization of his thoughts. At which point thought itself ceased.

So it went, day in day out. Life in paradise settled into a routine. The superlative degree of all that is fine and good became dreadfully familiar. After dining on ambrosia for days on end, he came to appreciate what the standardization of perfection meant. Nothing was relative any more; as soon as the gratification of one desire threatened to overshadow some other desire, that other desire was the one that was immediately fulfilled. It drove him crazy! When he deliberately refused his food in order to recapture the feeling of hunger, it turned out that he only ate for enjoyment, but as soon as he refused his food so as to deprive himself of that enjoyment, it turned out that he only ate from habit. His final attempt to feel something, anything, was to order an interactive hologram. The program was entitled 'Live Dangerously'. (Scenes retouched.)

One day the flunkey came to his bed and announced: 'Sir, there's been some sort of administrative error. You are not dead after all. I'm afraid you'll have to return to our branch on earth.'

WITHOUT LOVE

Hungry?
A snack...
Sleepless?
A mogadon...
Down?
Prozac...
Tired?
An upper...
Hyper?
A beta blocker...
Frightened?
A silent alarm...
Slow?
A high-speed train...
Hot?
A smart house...
Thirsty?
A smart drink...
Dirty?
An ethnic cleaner...
Harried?
A weekend retreat...
Chilly?
A House Automation System...
Predictable?
A survival course...
Damaged?
A prothesis..
Undamaged?
A prothesis anyway...
Dull?
A house party...
Small world?
Internet...
And so on and so forth.

SMART ≠ INTELLIGENT

REVIVAL OR SURVIVAL

IN A TROUBLE-FREE ZONE

(WHERE THE QUESTION IS POSED AS TO WHETHER THE IDEAL OF MORAL, BIOLOGICAL AND ARCHITECTURAL WEIGHTLESSNESS IS THE ULTIMATE IDEAL.)

There is no reason why the role of the computer should end with the material realization of this architecture. Quite the reverse, in fact, for computers can be used to control not only the production of an environment but also the way we experience that environment. Although we label such computer-controlled environments 'intelligent', this should not be taken as an indication of superiority. For between stupidity and genius are many kinds of intelligence.

What is an intelligent building? As everyone who has ever pondered the notion of 'intelligence' is aware, it depends on how you measure it. There is no such thing as straightforward intelligence. Nor, of course, has such a building anything to do with intellectual capacity. Perhaps an intelligence quotient would be nearer the mark. It's possible to imagine an architectural intelligence test which would measure buildings on a scale from simple Simon to clever Dick. The highest score would go to the building that is actually one vast database, capable of rapidly processing a constant stream of people, goods and information; it would have an ingenious program and also be durable and economical. A system so intelligent that people no longer notice the transition to the outside world; an environment that eschews identity and hence also IQ tests. Not that such a building has ever seen the light. What has been built to date is not much more than a collection of high-tech gadgets.

The trouble with a phenomenon that lacks a recognizable identity on a well defined façade is that it doesn't have a lot to show for itself. Let me at least give a brief rundown of what is currently conceivable. I think of this intelligent master-system as a combination of a) TRON (Real Time Operating System Nucleus) House technology (based on a model project by Ken Sakamura), incorporating every comfort-enhancing device you can think of: from clothing tips (depending on the weather and your wardrobe) to bathroom fittings that monitor your state of health; b) security technology guaranteed to eliminate break-ins and fires; c) on-line connections to a wide range of environments so as to banish any sense of monasticism: this would not be limited to graphic information but would also include olfactory, **page 39** auditory and tactile data. d) potential self-sufficiency due to sun collectors, biomass processing, wind turbines and the like; e) smart materials that facilitate extensive flexibility and which have the power to enhance experience; f) funware operated by remote control or speech recognition; g) LCD technology which is sensitive to molecular movements, thus making it possible to transfer every conceivable type of information and aesthetic effect; h) climatic control and building maintenance embracing everything from automatic switch-offs to human-presence detectors.

For the present moment, this is all a bit premature. Even the most intelligent buildings are still at the autiste savant stage: quite staggering until you get to know them a bit better, at which point the trick starts to pall. Given that virtually all intelligence is presently being directed towards manipulating people, air, light, goods and information and that very little effort is being invested in enhancing expressive and programmatic intelligence, I shall stick to the following definition for the time being: an intelligent building is a house with no style. It is possible that such a building would be positively unsightly. Or that there might not even be anything to see.

On the other hand, all the more to experience. Of course we could always react to discussions about intelligent buildings with raised eyebrows and questions as to the feasibility. Deliberately provocative questions such as: Wouldn't it be better if people themselves lived more intelligently, if need be in stupid houses? Do you honestly expect to meet the light of your life in such an intelligent, narcissistic machine? Who's going to have charge of the remote control? Likewise, who's going to preside over all that stored data, in particular the security system data? And do you really want your smart lavatory warning you that you only have a short time to live? Have you worked out the cost of maintenance? Delicate questions, indeed. Yet despite all the cynicism it is difficult to ignore the fact that applications based on artificial intelligence are poised to hit the mass market. For that matter, what is 'authentic' intelligence anyway? Small wonder that the adjective 'artificial' is increasingly omitted nowadays.

Several favourable conditions (for the industry, that is) are about to become decisive. They would be more likely to inspire confidence if market research were to focus more on specific target groups. One huge unexplored area is that of care for the elderly, which is going to find itself under increasing pressure as the percentage of elderly people rises. Given the appropriate supporting functions and teleservices, they would be able to remain in their own homes a lot longer. A second opening lies in the growth of one-person households and the rise in the number of busy two-income couples, both needing efficiency-enhancing and time-saving technologies. Thirdly, strong environmental pressure represents a marvellous opportunity for domotica. And finally, there is the growth of the private housing sector. Private home ownership, as part of a condominium or otherwise, is on the increase, bringing with it a new demand for security technology in particular. In short, these are all durable, long term developments which make the large-scale application of domotica well nigh inevitable. The time is ripe for 'thinking in terms of plug-and-play interior systems'.

This essay at any rate assumes that the actual implementation of this new technology has already taken place: the trend towards computer-controlled living, working, recreation and communication is sufficiently real to permit a few bold speculations. After all, behind these trends lie far more sweeping historical changes, that are currently taking place and that we would do well to take into account when exploring strategies for the future, rather than dismissing them as social-historical hobbyhorses.

In our long-distance telelifestyle where everything is nonetheless close at hand and instantly available, we no longer believe in what have come to be known as romantic clichés - by which I mean the rhetorical formulas that enabled us to accept human inadequacy. 'No pain, no gain' but now nothing hurts anymore. The only things being created nowadays are favourable conditions. It is said that 'inspiration equals perspiration' but the Home Binary Unit System makes perspiration obsolete. How inspiration is to be evaluated from now on is something we'll worry about tomorrow. The environment with the impeccable 'flexible response', the building that fits you like a tailor-made 'datasuit', never remains the same. It gives new meaning to Heraclitus's dictum that 'you can't step twice into the same river'. For river read intelligent environment. Freed of all those philosophical essences relating to the 'idea' of the house and the ontology of territory that have dogged us from Plato to Heidegger, we find ourselves back in a pre-Socratic universe where nothing lays claim to eternity. The truly intelligent house is a permanently changing context that has as many manifestations as there are combinations of an infinite number of variables. In other words, an infinite number of manifestations. That's going to involve a lot of searching. Don't go out without your notebook and digital route planner.

YOU DON'T USE TECHNOLOGY ANY MORE,
YOU ARE TECHNOLOGY

Not so very long ago artificial intelligence was wont to appear in the guise of an opponent. Remember digital chess? Since then the computer has changed from adversary to best friend. The allocation of chip addresses to everything worth manipulating has turned the computer into living matter; has made it, in a sense, part of us. The machine was an extension of our limbs; but the computer? We are an extension of it. No wonder we love it. After all, who's going to amputate bits of themselves? Long live the symbiosis with the motherboard! Only with digitization has the fusion between organic and mechanical become a real possibility.

Yet if technology has indeed become part of us, it is only logical that it should be invisible. If not literally so, in the form of built-in protheses - the architecturally integrated concealment of terminals and the mechanics of remote-control - then figuratively, in that we simply don't notice the technology any more. So interwoven is it with daily life that it has become one with it. And whether our environment will end up being managed from the top down by a highly hierarchical control system or whether, on the contrary, it will come to resemble a horizontal mesh-work, the world of machines and appliances is making way for wide-spread computer-backed sensor technology, for a field of intersections. Technology is less and less about things, more and more about environment.

For architecture this conclusion is more or less crucial to its continued existence, at least, in a material sense. Which is why designers at the cutting edge of architectural practice talk increasingly about helping to create 'events' rather than about making objects. This is no autonomous aesthetic or programmatic preference, an expression of free will on the part of a few isolated architects. The fact is that architecture is in the process of losing its age-old mandate to generate space, create places, to separate here from there, and very few architects appear to have realized this. A whole range of architectural and urban types, from the bank to the pizza parlour, which at one time would have entailed an automatic territorial claim, are now in the process of dissolving. The relationship between outer appearance, programmatic functions, infrastructure and electronic networks is in a state of flux and architects might just - it is only a suggestion, mind - play a major role in pondering and guiding this reorganization.

THE MORE INTELLIGENT THE BETTER

It is well known that nomadic peoples often have highly intelligent dwellings. I myself once visited a Lahu community in Indo-China, where the one living area accommodated at least two social dimensions. Those in the official dimension (front entrance), simply did not see what went on in the unofficial dimension (back entrance). This mental construct made it possible for parents and children to pursue their lives side by side without constantly getting in one another's hair. Physically adjacent worlds were kept mentally separate. Lives lived in physical proximity were perceived mentally as two separate worlds.

It is surely no coincidence that with the end of our sedentary existence and the return of a sort of nomadism (bringing with it a certain deterritorialization), the future of architecture should hang on concepts like flexibility and impermanence. The difference is that instead of looking to the human imagination to provide that flexibility, we are now intent on making the human environment easy to dismantle and portable. Not that this should be interpreted as an anthropological circle come full turn. The emergence of the intelligent environment is best seen as the natural consequence of several linear historical processes. Reference has already been made to the insatiable human desire for more comfort, more security and more amusement. This desire can become so intense that human-ness itself is called into question. Exit condition humaine. In this reading, human inadequacy is a thing of the past, not because that inadequacy has been eliminated, but because we are in the post-human era. Or is that perhaps the same thing?

But there are other reasons behind the push towards an intelligent environment. There are those, for instance, who are so alarmed by the yawning differences in wealth, culture and mentality, that they would like to raise the dividing walls even higher. Artificial intelligence, in the form of advanced surveillance circuits, could help them to do this. Furthermore, the high degree of specialization in modern society tends to leave people feeling responsible for only one aspect of society, seldom for the whole lot. The result is splendid transport corridors, splendid nature reserves, splendid housing enclaves, splendid theme parks, splendid protected historical cityscapes and splendid industrial areas, while the area in-between, the so-called public domain, is a sorry remnant for which no one takes any responsibility. This is the fate of networks: the intersections are well cared for, the bits in-between languish.

Of course the intelligent environment, certainly on an urban scale, is also a spatial manifestation of economic and technological innovations. Just as high-rise waited upon the invention of the lift, and the functional city can be seen as a spatial expression of Fordism, so the progressive dismantling of material architecture can be interpreted as a result of digitization and Soft City, as a symbol of the flexible capital of late capitalism. In this sense Modernism could perhaps be said to be notching up yet another success, if not in form, then certainly in letter and spirit, for the Modernist ideal of lightness and transparency, flexibility and dynamism is destined to shape the environment in the 21st century, too. To such an extent that one might claim, with slight exaggeration, that the environment as such will make way for a field of interactivity which may not even need the addition of a spatially integrative framework. There will no longer be any 'there', only a 'here'. And a 'now', of course, that goes without saying.

In fact, it is not only the ideals of 'classic' Modernists like Le Corbusier or Alexander Dorner that will be realized; but also those of the anti-authoritarian and anti-territorial generation of the Sixties. The dreams of Buckminster Fuller, Constant Nieuwenhuys, Hans Hollein, Nicolaas Habraken, Cedric Price, Future Systems, Toyo Ito and the early Rem Koolhaas will also become reality. Although I'm very much afraid that this heaven on earth will be produced not by architecture but by services engineering. A distinction that will by then, of course, scarcely matter.

Apart from the pursuit of lightness, transparency and flexibility, there is one other characteristic of the intelligent environment reminiscent of Modernism. It is the emphasis on 'facilitative' conditions. Just as with the Modern Movement's neutral isotropic space, the enthusiasm for the smart space is all about the life and events that space makes possible. Architecture provides the podium, it's up to people to make the most of it. Which is another way of saying that this architecture is based on the idea of negative freedom, which is supposed to lead to a positive use of that freedom. But as we have already seen with Modernism, things don't always work out as planned. Just as The Language of Post Modern Architecture, with its numerous allegorical and decorative additions to the modern shell, can be seen as a reaction to Modernism's scary neutral emptiness, the odds are that instead of 'facilitating' a richer way of life, full of interesting 'events', artificial intelligence will send people scrambling for figurative virtual reality scenarios with which to fill the void.

As long as the facilitating policy of negative freedom was accompanied by a fairly serious desire to use that freedom to achieve something in life, the belief in a perfectible society could remain intact. The intelligent environment, too, would have its quota of independent-minded individuals, with still more time for a still more meaningful life. But we could be forgiven for asking who on earth is interested in this, if 'meaning' means instant satisfaction.

In sum, the current impetus for the intelligent environment comes from a wide variety of sources: social and economic conditions; digital technology's capacity to transmit visual and auditory information with almost no costs, zap from one piece of information to another, store it safely and navigate its way through it all by means of efficient interfaces; the Enlightenment dream of emancipation and our perennial disgust with human inadequacy - they all come together in the SMART world.

A   GREAT   AND   COMPELLING   LIFE
IN   A   PARADISE   FOR   THE   PAINSHY

One wonders whether something so dependent on context, interactivity and interface can still be called a building. In any event, not in the sense of a materially delineated volume, designed and set down by a particular professional calling him or herself an architect. When it comes to building an intelligent structure where the 'detachable unit' is more important than the 'structural support', where aspects such as adjacency and materiality are no longer relevant and where the job of technical engineer or facility manager has more to do with creativity than that of architect, it is clear that the latter's intelligence will be found to be obsolete. Those architects who are sufficiently determined to survive will find themselves increasingly working with interfaces rather than making things. With engineers rather than as lonely geniuses. Architecture will become an organizational art.

In one respect such an architecture will represent the triumph of the avant-garde ideal of 'self-referentiality'. In the last instance, a building that is no more than a self-referring system, rather than a metaphor for something else, is totally self-contained. Even the decorated shed is a completely outdated concept; like the ancient sun temple, it always refers to something else. A building with a pronounced façade is still busy sending out a signal, which also serves to emphasize its boundary. But a building conceived as a 'field' no longer sends out signals. One does not communicate with such a building, it communicates with itself.

In another respect, however, the dullest version of this type of architecture is proof of the failure of that same avant-garde, for despite its frantic attempts to integrate architecture with life, it has nothing more profound to say about that life than that it should be efficient and perhaps 'dynamic'. And lo and behold, with a bit of son et lumière, it works. Now the couch potato can revert to pure protoplasm. While everything else is in the process of becoming immaterial, light and mobile, there we sit in our media rooms in a state of total inertia, counting sheep in an effort to sleep away the centuries of boredom. And here we have just one more modern paradox: at the very moment when technology makes it possible for us to do anything we like, we're bored with novelty.

And yet... There is another version; an artificial intelligence that does not replace our own intelligence but enhances it; that instead of anaesthetizing and ultimately replacing the senses, creates a world which offers a richer mix of experience. It is an intelligence that complements human intelligence rather than contending with it and it implies a completely different approach to the experience of smart, interactive spaces than that offered by domotica. The environments it produces will be anything but neutralizing; far from relieving the senses they will in fact place additional demands on them. Such environments, designed by programmers who ignore the dictates of the market and follow instead their own inclinations in applying smart-tech, might turn architecture into an interactive Gesamtkunstwerk. Even if this means that matter loses its primacy, there is no need to fear that the body will be reduced to the status of a mollusc. Quite the contrary. This kind of environment calls for individuals who are in more than full command of their senses.

If architecture is to become an organizational art, then it is also time to ask, what kind of organization? Artificial intelligence requires intelligent artificiality. It's about time we had a course of training for this and, more importantly, a practice of building.

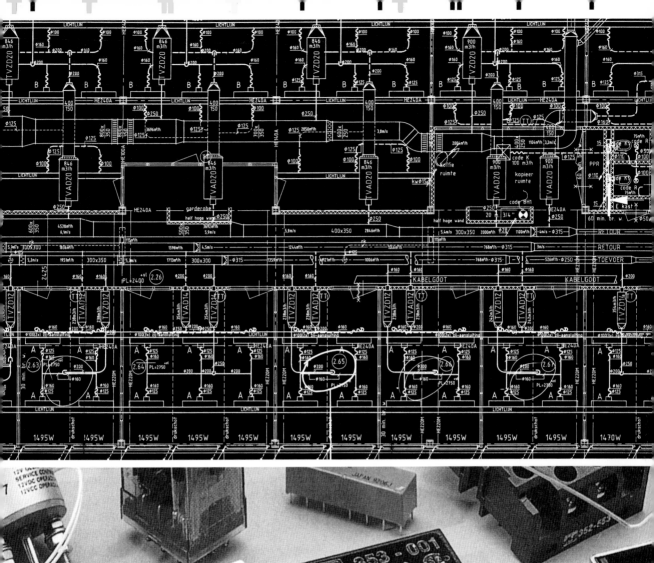

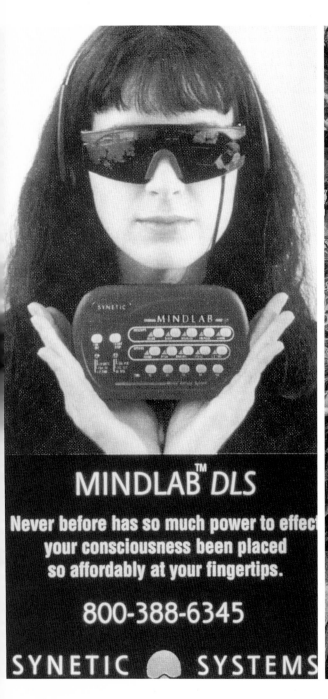

REALSPACE, QUICKTIME AND ARCHITECTURE

(WHETHER POSING QUESTIONS MAKES ANY SENSE IN VR)

The last two chapters dealt with the computer's role in producing (CAD) and experiencing (SMART-tech) the physical, material environment. A worst-case combination of these two applications would lead to predictable standardized construction and an environment where wealth of experience is sacrificed to higher productivity and efficiency. Architecture is then no more than an assembled building kit equipped with a building management system. At its best such a CAD/SMART combination would lead to nothing less than a new and glorious episode in the history of architecture. CAD technology makes possible a radical design overhaul, a spatial game beside which even Piranesi would pale into insignificance. The resulting space would be able to accommodate an artificial intelligence that enhances experience rather than neutralizing it. An intelligence which, instead of anticipating desires for safety, comfort and economy, responds to human intelligence.

Nor does the computer's role end here. It is also capable of mediating experiences which no longer require the existence of a real building. The cybernetic environment becomes virtual. This is what is meant by virtual reality (VR): the production and experience of totally simulated environments. Projected improvements in bandwidth, resolution and the speed of data processing suggest that whereas today's virtual reality products are regarded as mere surrogates, in future they will be preferred to the real thing. But we're not there yet. And the question remains whether the contracting out of human imagination is a cause for much rejoicing.

Virtual reality is an umbrella term that covers a wide variety of meanings. The idea of a virtual world - in the sense of recreated reality - dates as far back as the paintings in the Lascaux caves and ever since the discovery of linear perspective during the Renaissance, Western cultural history in particular has been full of 'lifelike' representations. Even the idea of the Wunderkammer is quite old. Accordingly, the latest wave of simulations, **page 47** whether they are experienced in VR booths or under HMDs (head-mounted display units), can be seen as part of a long-standing tradition of ooh and aah. Nor, finally, is VR in the form of a rhetorical gesture exactly new; every classical rhetorician dreamed of a synthesis of logos, pathos and mythos. Seen in this light, virtual reality is simply a continuation of an old tradition using new, digital tools.

There is, however, good reason for maintaining that this tradition is now entering a new phase that will change its very nature. It is no longer a matter of a short-lived simulation of reality for adjuration, education or pleasure, but of actually creating that reality. Once this has been done with any degree of success, the original can be discarded, at which moment virtual reality will become virtuality. No longer a fleeting representation, but a general, permanent condition. The dialectic between real and unreal will be a thing of the past.

But we've a long way to go yet before we reach that point. There's a difference between VR in the form of applicable technology and VR as a utopian ambition, and there is no consensus as to whether these two will ever become one. Indeed, some people regard VR as at best a practical aid in developing prototypes and/or for putting together attractive presentations and that's as far as they want it to go. For others, however, VR represents the realization of a perfect world where the Creation can be repeated from scratch, but this time on our terms. They regard today's fairly schematic form of VR, which provides mere animations of environments that may one day really 'come to life', and where people just practice for the real world, as no more than a crude foretaste of the '21st century' or 'the Third Millennium', when VR will make full-blown teleliving possible. And more! When we live in the electro-unit, we will log in to an on-line world that will provide us with everything we now have to go out and fetch for ourselves. The two most important elements of VR, interaction and immersion, will then have become absolute. Everything will be compatible. The eye, which now enjoys primacy in every VR environment, will be supported by the other senses, including the sixth. For the present, though, such a picture belongs largely to the realms of the imagination.

Despite the huge discrepancy between fact and fiction, VR dominates the current world view. The technical realization of VR is less important than our intense preoccupation with it. There are a number of facets to this preoccupation and it is these I would now like to address.

THE PRICE OF PROGRESS

The economy is riding high, the deciduous forests are recovering and public violence appears to be declining. The statistics are cheerful. The big problems concerning the earth have scarcely any relevance to daily life. The crux of the matter - that we pursue infinite progress with finite resources - is so abstract that it cannot serve as a guide for anyone, and certainly not for those whose responsibility is chopped into four-year terms.

In the meanwhile, our modern-day Cassandras have not been idle. For those who make society their study it has long been obvious that such universal principles as freedom, mobility, self-realization, equality, self-determination, the pursuit of happiness, freedom of speech, the right to shelter, individualism, curiosity, adventurousness, voluntarism and so on, have their limits. In recent times this has been increasingly expressed in terms of an abstract limiting factor indicating the extent to which we must reduce our consumption of natural resources in order to achieve 'sustainability'. At present we are at 'factor 20'; in a few years time we will have reached factor 30. And so on, right up to Stunde Null. It's a neat way of reducing an necessary ecological revolution to a simple mathematical problem, but essentially what it says is that in RealSpace the price of Enlightenment ideals is simply too high. The Great Revolution is going to require more than mathematics. Or perhaps not. If that mathematics is binary, perhaps something can be done after all. Can the computer save the world?

aforecited Enlightenment ideals. Not only was architecture as organized space a rewarding metaphor for the positivist conquest of the world, but architecture as a material order was also directly involved in the gigantic consumption of space, the environment and resources entailed by the process of modernization. (A total moratorium on architecture would in itself result in a dramatic reduction of that factor 20.) Perhaps the price of architecture has become too high for the continuing emancipation of humanity.

The most obvious response is: no more emancipation then. Yet quite apart from the question of whether that would not be a negation of history, it is simply inconceivable. As Adam Smith already realized, emancipation is the only acceptable justification for capitalism's endless expansion and innovation. In VR, however, (late) capitalism could carry on without fatal consequences.

VR, then, is a New Frontier, a luminous reworking of the time-honoured notion of 'Go West'. Once a three-dimensional grid has been laid over the real earth, culminating in the global village, a new universe will emerge where the explorer mentality will find new employment. The Frontier was never a real target but rather psychological compensation for the death of the great watchmaker. Insofar as cyberspace is a terra incognita, a place where everything is still beautiful and unspoilt, it is an Ersatz for paradise. The only pity is that the process of mapping and conquering this realm all too often goes hand in hand with the disciplining and impoverishment of the real world.

So there is good reason for asking which values (intimacy, compassion, solidarity, community spirit, etc.) we must renounce and to what extent VR really can deliver further emancipation. Is not the imposition of discipline and stupidity inherent in the very structure of virtuality? Be that as it may, ignoring VR will not get us very far either. Instead of abandoning this sector of cyberspace to producers who promise to banish boredom, solve problems and sell services, we would do better to turn our attention to VR as a dimension in which it is possible to think and to develop new ideas. This project is still very much in its infancy.

LIVE LIKE A SPARTAN, FEEL LIKE CALIGULA

In order to make people more willing to embark on this project, we must first discard a number of durable psychological processes. It is striking how loudly people talk of 'freedom' in connection with the introduction of systems constructed strictly according to rules. When all's said and done, digitales are logarithmical and protocol-driven. Although some VR offers a refined simulation of a world that is free from time, place and personal identity, and to some extent succeeds in bringing the divine privileges of infinity, immortality and omniscience within reach, one would be hard put to see the average computer devotee as a model of independent behaviour. On the contrary, his (occasionally her) freedom amounts to choosing from a menu bar. The great attraction of cyberspace lies precisely in the strict rules applying to every action. There's no getting around the fact that computers work with programs and that these are seldom written by visionaries. Another important mechanism standing in the way of a truly liberated use of the computer, is the abiding need to see cyberspace as a sort of latter-day Carnival and the cyborg as a latter-day grotesque. The posthumanist android can just as easily be seen as a premodern Rabelaisian figure who is not opposed to the world but one with it. VR becomes the domain of a reborn, medieval innocence. VR as a land of plenty is an upside-down world of waste, a social outlet, a mythical universe. Just as the VR Electronic Frontier can be seen as providing some compensation for the impending ecological reckoning, so the VR Carnival can be seen as compensation for an impending diet that will make Lent look like gluttony. Must we really economize to the tune of factor 20? Then at least let us do it in the Orgasmatron. It's

Thoughts do not have to be expressed through words or images in a given symbolic order; they can be 'experienced' without benefit of mediation. And be honest, wouldn't this be the ultimate fulfilment of the wisdom of Blaise Pascal, who said: 'All the misfortunes of men derive from one single thing, which is their inability to be at ease in a room.' VR allows you to scour the galaxies and still be back in time for tea.

The preprogrammed actions associated with the current interfaces on the one hand, and the carnivalesque relationship with the computer on the other, constitute pretty stiff obstacles to a self-confident, critical and creative use of the possibilities offered by VR. The only hope of a breakthrough on this front is a change in approach, most likely forced through by a new breed of operators. We need to stop seeing VR as a new 'medium' and view it as the next and crucial step in the cultural process of digitization. Instead of wondering whether or not to adopt the new medium, creative minds bursting with ideas could then address themselves to their relationship to a cultural process that is destined to shape the present era. In this respect, a reallocation of available talent is urgently needed.

PARADIGM SHIFT

The 'digitization' process not only confronts us with new means of communication but also with the consequences of those means for our world view. On the one hand these consequences do not look all that serious. The old familiar perspectival, homocentric view of things is more powerful than ever in VR and there are countless protocols and conditions that must be satisfied. In addition, it is clear that the insights of the major thinkers of the last 150 years - including Marx, Nietzsche, Freud and Einstein - have scarcely penetrated the VR domain. Cartesian logic is the order of the day.

On the other hand VR undeniably entails a paradigm shift. VR is not a 'found' world, but the invention of computer programmers. Instead of a life 'after nature', VR in principle is a world according to a mental projection. As such it is circumscribed by what goes on in the minds of those programmers. And to date this has clearly been of an almost exclusively Cartesian order. But it does not have to stay that way. Here indeed lies the germ of genuine innovation.

The designers of VR are usually preoccupied with how it works rather than how it should be. The program writer's engineering outlook is reminiscent of the cool gaze of the neurophysiologists whose analyses of, say, neocortex, hypothalamus, limbic system, Papez's circuit and the synapses and neurotransmissions in between, have given us a pretty good picture of what goes on up top. The secret of thought processes has been made visible to such an extent now that there is no longer any need to speculate about the ghost in the machine. The ghost exists and proof of its existence has been provided by computerized tomography of X-ray pictures (CT), positron emission tomography (PET scans) and magnetic resonance imaging (MRI). Whether you want something, remember something, analyse or feel something, they can see you thinking. (They being the men and women in white coats, of course.) Psychic phenomena and telepathy have had their day. Computer animations have now helped to demonstrate that the inventors of those same animations possess an anima.

Well then, it is this anima that dominates most VR productions. They are simply the products of the analytical minds that have applied themselves to reality, something that should be borne in mind when assessing the cultural value of VR. It is quite likely that if this technology were to be controlled by other minds, the nature of VR would change dramatically. VR might then extend beyond electronic mimesis to encompass independent ideas. At such a moment VR would no longer compensate an inevitable absence of individual imagination and judgement; instead it would be a medium that gives free play to a whole range of good and not-so-good qualities. To the extent that there is a 'challenge', this is where it's at.

dialectic of the Enlightenment. Nor is it possible to say with any

certainty that it will not. It would not be the first time that technology was expected to provide a solution to problems that are primarily a matter of mentality. But if we are determined to follow this course into uncharted waters, then let it not be in the sole company of agressive conquerors intent on staking a claim to their new territory as soon as possible, but rather together with those who possess sufficient civility, openness to possibilities and nomadic wonderment.

SPACE, TIME AND ARCHITECTURE IN VR

Can architecture go virtual? If so, how? If not, will it survive the digital revolution? It seems to me to come down to an academic question of definition. The fact is that VR has a role to play both in maintaining historical and existing architecture and in future construction. Both entail momentous consequences for our sense of nearness and our experience of the environment.

1) Until recently, if you wanted to know what your country looked like in the past or how it might have looked, you had to rely on your own powers of imagination sparked off by drawings and photos in a wide array of architectural publications. But suppose you had no imagination. In that case the existing literature would not have been much help. However fine the pictures, however exhaustively the buildings are documented in four-colour prints, the spatial play of architecture is the exclusive preserve of material reality.

Now, however, it is possible to imagine a databank, a super hologram, where a country could be transformed at will into the desired built environment, albeit a VR environment. The visitor would be able to choose from a lavish inventory of structures that can in fact no longer be visited, but which he or she can now walk around as if they were real. This would also be a sensible way of spending cultural heritage funds, goals such as preservation and popularization would be dealt with in one fell swoop. Commission a specialized firm to virtualize Duiker's Zonnestraal Sanatorium and not only would the government save millions on the preservation and maintenance of the building, it would also make this Nieuwe Bouwen monument accessible to countless numbers of people. What's more, the same government could make money selling the rights, while at the same time avoiding an endless stream of tourists heading for Hilversum. Profit all round. And that's not the end of it: the entire history of architecture can be put on-line. It is simply a question of time and feeding in the data. There is already a growing database containing the wonders of the world and the monuments on the World Heritage List. If you surf the Internet with 'Virtual Tourist', you can already visit quite a number of the world's great cities. And should you happen to know the password for the CIA Intelink program, and hence have a direct link to the spy satellite network, you can see everything in real time which is on an architectural scale. Access to everything from one central computer terminal, plus the theoretically endless digital reproduction and distribution of everything cultural, adds up to a decisive development in our relationship with the world around us. The past = the present. The far-off is the here. In such circumstances there is an urgent need to undermine the tendency towards slavish reproduction of what is past or far-off with self-willed 'interactivity'. That is to say that within the documentary, ready-made nature of the images called up, the user should retain a certain room to manoeuvre, to follow his/her own agenda. It is of course vital that the quality of this agenda should be well developed from an early age by means of training in digital literacy.

2) As far as the future is concerned there are two possibilities for architecture, once again depending on what you understand by architecture. A) Architecture will restrict itself to the material environment and accept its modest role in a multi-player system governed by market forces. (Apart from the familiar exceptions to the rule.) Its critical task, for example, would then consist of being as economical as possible in its use of resources, although this also is an objective that is all too liable to be interpreted in favour of the market. B) Architecture will extend the definition

making of all kinds of environments, including digital ones.

The first scenario signifies the end of a historical cycle. Architecture will loose its indispensability as a separate discipline. The second scenario offers architecture a second lease of life for centuries to come. No matter which direction the time-space concept takes we are still going to find ourselves inhabiting 'environments'. More than ever before we are going to have to learn to find our way around these environments, we are going to be following unfamiliar, multidimensional paths. Those architects who address themselves to the new technology should strive for optimum conceptual clarity. But movement through this virtual space is not the only concern. The quality of the 'accommodation' - compared with what is presently available - can also be vastly improved. The VR of the future will not be restricted to finding and passing on edutainment; it will be possible to create places similar to the major historical architectural types. From places of worship to casinos, from prisons to music theatres, every function has a potential virtual version. Architecture today is minimally prepared for this new mandate. Meagre capital, meagre know-how and meagre confidence lead to meagre innovation. On the other hand, the new field of activity is ready and waiting. The dramatic growth of cyberspace makes it increasingly easy to 'just start somewhere'. The only real problem is a chronic lack of time. Almost all developments in this field are brought about by people who are paid - i.e. given the time - to do just that. Lack of time is the greatest obstacle to a versatile, creative and alternative use of the computer.

To sum up: the material environment is losing its significance vis-à-vis the new electronic dimensions where an increasing part of the action is. So long as architecture is seen as a pure service profession it does not have much to offer in this new context and the designing of Cyberia will continue to be left to computer engineers and marketing men. So far this state of affairs has produced not much more than market-oriented schematic clichés. But if, in addition to taking their role of service provider seriously, architects were also to aspire to the role of expeditionary leader, a magnificent future would open up. Software engineering and interface design are all areas where an architectural perspective could make a vital contribution. Architects of all dimensions, there is an immense amount of work to be done!

FROM THE PHILOSOPHER'S STONE

There is a chemical version of Electronic VR which, though not much talked of by engineers, is socially speaking every bit as important. Only relatively few people have so far seen a Silicon Graphics Reality Engine at close quarters, but millions exist on a daily diet of psychoactive drugs that serve to simulate various states of mind. Electronic VR appeals mainly to the eye and even the simplest application requires a sizeable chunk of machinery. Allopathic and alternative medicines, on the other hand, affect all levels of consciousness without a trace of hardware. Nevertheless, while their manner of manipulating the senses is beyond the power of the computer, they could never have been developed in the first place without computerized neuropsychological research. Architectural criticism of these drugs is hampered by the fact that the closer one gets to the object of study, the more one's objectivity declines. What follows should therefore not be seen as a closely-reasoned analysis, but as an attempt to say something worthwhile about the subliminal effects of smart drugs.

Smart drugs are pills and powders to live in. A lot of research still needs to be done into the precise relationship between various cocktails of endogenous and exogenous substances and the sense of being at home, of being safe, or the very opposite, the tendency to extraversion and mental adventurousness. The fact remains, however, that with a bit of fantasy it is possible to imagine a palette of architectural styles corresponding to the main groups of psychoactive drugs. Prozac, XTC, MDMA, MDM, DMT, Adam X, M-Ethyl are the lubricants of the neurotransmission system. Now that we know that a pleasant sensation is all a matter of chemistry, all we have to do is to reconstruct that chemistry. Including, of course, euphoria and divine ecstasy. Now everybody can aspire to transcendence; it is merely a question of the right ingredients in the right proportions.

Panic attack? Anxiety, aggression or territorial paranoia? MDMA can temporarily suspend the brain circuits responsible for such destructive feelings. Away with them! DMT (dimethyl tryptamine) is even more potent; it is nothing less than a psychoactive virtual reality. A DMT trip is the perfect preparation for the forthcoming hyperdimensional, timeless, impersonal reality. And XTC, of course, will have you automatically describing these fantastic fractals on the dance floor during houseraves. Or what do you say to taking Vasopressin for complicated programmatic and organizational hitches in your private databank (formerly known as your life story); suddenly you can see things in perspective again. If your life is too fraught, dose yourself with Piracetam or Pyroglutamate for tension and acute stress. Next, as a precaution against a relapse, take Hydergine as a prophylactic for chronic stress. And finally, when your supreme happiness has made you so universally attractive that you are invited everywhere, there's L-tyrosine for permanent jet lag.

Make no mistake, life in the computer age won't be all smooth sailing. Complicated system management, identity and gender bending, philosophical and spiritual expeditions to the furthest corners of the Internet, Netpals who suddenly disappear, a stressful working environment or a creative dip: the road to heaven will be no bed of roses. It's just as well that there are smart drugs.

It's not the good people who go to heaven, but the smart ones.

TO THE PHILOSOPHER IS STONED

THE SIMILE

Enter the chilly no-man's land. For adult cave life. No additional drugs required. All senses operative.

That's something I learned to my cost! Upon entering the Chill Cave - a gloomy crypt underneath the building - I was first allowed to spend some time in the anteroom, attended by the hostess on duty. A glass of hot sake helped to warm me up. The cavern contained two prototypes of the Chill Terminal where I would presently be able to partake of mind-expanding videos. The idea was that I would surrender myself to video drugs, the adult brain grooves. And suchlike.

After chatting a little about the future of such cellars as a serious means of combatting stress (in Japan they are subsidized by large corporations) it was time to get down to business. The hostess beckoned me to follow and a curtain was drawn away in front of me. I stepped into the inner sanctum of the profane, into the shrine of the Great Void, in short, into the gloom of Plato's cave turned opium den. Warm from the sake, my heart pounding in anticipation, I sank down onto one of the mattresses, my head level with the video tunnel suspended above me. I looked into the shaft and saw that its walls were covered with mirrors ending in a monitor screen. The monitor was still blank.

A second later I felt a searing pain in my shoulders. My escort had lowered the massively heavy device without first checking on my position. The edge of the shaft pressed me deep into the mattress; my collarbone gave a loud crack. I was shackled to the hardware.

With a supreme effort I managed to wriggle half free of the machine and while I was still recovering from the shock, I was suddenly bombarded with images. All senses operative, that much I had expected, but that the sense of touch could so override the sense of sight was something I had not supposed possible. The eye's evolutionary advantage was wiped out by the lacerations I was aware of under my clothing. And although these shoulders were strong enough to bear the wealth of images, you'll understand me when I say that from that moment onwards it was all over with my critic's objectivity.

How many images did I see? I've no idea now, nor do I recollect the slightest meaning. It was all movement and sound in countless variations, but programmed with all the orderliness of a bead kaleidoscope.

I survived the psychedelics, in panavision and sensurround. I'm okay, you're okay. I surfed on the ripples of the Void. I was spared delirium, delusion and hallucinosis. And I thought:

Imagine someone, once freed from the clutches of the dream, descending again to his former cave and resuming his old place. Would his eyes not be filled with darkness, coming in so suddenly from the sun? And imagine that he were to engage in a competition with those who had remained there all along, to see who was best at deciphering the shadows - wouldn't he cut a poor figure, while his sight was still clouded? They would claim that the journey upwards, to the sun, had cost him his eyes and that you'd have to be crazy to undertake such a trip towards the light. Wouldn't they be inclined to murder anyone who wanted to deliver them from their cave and lead them to the light?

Undoubtedly. For in their cavernous eyes the darkness has eclipsed the light. And the light comprehended it not.

OF THE CAVE

ARCHITECTS

OF ALL DIMENSIONS,

THERE IS

AN IMMENSE

AMOUNT   OF   WORK

TO BE DONE!

INDEX

BIBLIOGRAPHY

DIGISOPHY

Books:

Agricola, E., Gieling, L., Wagenaar, C. (red.), Archipolis over de grenzen van de architectuur, Studium Generale, Delft 1994.

Bender, G., Druckrey, T., Culture on the Brink. Ideologies of Technology, Bay Press, Seattle 1994.

Benedikt, M., Cyberspace; First Steps, MIT Press, Cambridge Massachusetts 1992.

Bolz, N., Am Ende der Gutenberg-galaxis. Die neuen Kommunikationsverhältnisse, Wilhelm Fink Verlag, München 1993.

Bouman, O., Toorn, R. van, The Invisible in Architecture, Academy Editions, London 1994.

Bukatman, S., Terminal Identity. The Virtual Subject in Postmodern Science Fiction, Duke University Press, London 1993.

Cotton, B., Oliver, R., Understanding Hypermedia. From Multimedia to Virtual Reality, Phaidon Press, London 1992.

Cotton, B., Oliver, R., The Cyberspace Lexicon, Phaidon Press, London 1994.

Cuperus, R., Hurenkamp, M. (red.), Nederland in 2025. Nuchtere toekomstbeelden van een nieuwe generatie, Wiardi Beckman Stichting, Amsterdam 1995.

Feireiss, K., Ben van Berkel. Mobile Forces/Mobile Kräfte, Ernst & Sohn, Berlin 1994.

Freiberger, P., McNeill, D., Fuzzy Logic. The Revolutionary Computer Technology that is changing our World, Simon & Schuster, New York 1993.

Friedland, R., Boden, D., NowHere: Space, Time and Modernity, University of California Press, London 1994.

Gerbel, K., Weibel P., Intelligente Ambiente. Intelligent Environment, Band 1, Band 2, (Festival für Kunst, Technologie und Gesellschaft), PVS Verleger, Wien 1994.

Gerbel, K., Weibel, P. (ed.), Mythos Information. Welcome to the Wired World, Ars Electronica 95, Springer - Verlag, Wien/New York 1995.

Heim, M., The Metaphysics of Virtual Reality, Oxford University Press, Oxford 1993.

Holtzman, S.R., Digital Mantras. The Languages of Abstract and Virtual Worlds, MIT Press, Cambridge Massachusetts 1994.

Landa, M. De, War in the Age of Intelligent Machines, Swerve, New York 1991.

Mitchell, W.J., City of Bits. Space, Place, and the Infobahn, MIT Press, Cambridge Massachusetts 1995.

Negroponte, N., Digitaal leven, Uitgeverij Prometheus, Amsterdam 1995.

Petrella, R., Grenzen aan de concurrentie, De groep van Lissabon, VUBpress, Brussel 1994.

Postman, N., Technopoly. The Surrender of Culture to Technology, Vintage Books, New York 1993.

Rheingold, H., The Virtual Community. Homestaeding on the Electronic Frontier, Addison-Wesley Publishing Company, Amsterdam 1993.

Rushkoff, D., Cyberia. Life in the Trenches of Hyperspace, HarperCollins Publishers, New York 1994.

Sassen, S., The Global City: New York, London, Tokyo, Princeton University Press, New York 1991.

Soja, E.W., Postmodern Geographies. The Reassertion of Space in Critical Social Theory, Verso, London/New York 1989.

Taylor, M.C., Saarinen E., Imagologies. Media Philosophy, Routledge, London 1994.

Teyssot, G., Diller, E., Scofidio, R., Flesh: Architectural Probes. The Mutant Body of Architecture, Princeton Architectural Press, New York 1994.

Magazines - theme issues:

ANY, Electrotecture: Architecture and the Electronic Future, nr. 3, 1993.

ANY, Mech in Tecture. Reconsidering the Mechanical in the Electronic Era, nr. 10, 1995.

De Architect, Maalstroom van de techniek, nr. 49, november 1992.

El Croquis, Ben van Berkel, nr. 72, 1995.

El Croquis, Toyo Ito 1986-1995, nr. 71, 1995.

Forum, Comfort, vol. 38, nr. 1/2, may 1995.

Kunstforum, Die Zukunft des Körpers, Bd. 132, November-Januar 1996.

Mediamatic, The 1/0 issue, vol. 7, nr. 1, winter 1992.

Mediamatic, The Storage Mania Issue, vol. 8, nr. 1, summer 1994.

NOX, Actiones in distans, Stichting Highbrow 1991.

NOX, Chloroform: een samenleving onder narcose, Stichting Highbrow 1993.

NOX, Djihad, Uitgeverij Duizend en Een, Amsterdam 1995.

Articles:

Boyer, C.M., 'De denkbeeldige reële wereld van de CyberCities', De Architect nr. 3, maart 1993, p. 25-37.

Deitch, J., 'Het einde van de mens', Wave nr. 3, juli/augustus 1994, p. 32-35.

Dery, M., 'ready for take off... Achterhaalde wezens en post-menselijke wezens', Wave nr.11, juni 1995, p. 57-63.

Nedervelde, P. van, 'Technologische singulariteit', Wave nr. 3, juli/augustus 1994, p. 85-86.

Perrella, S., 'Computer Imaging: Morphing and Architectural Representation', Architectural Design vol. 63, nr. 3/4, march/april 1993, p. 90.

Perrella, S., 'Interview with Mark Dippe: Terminator 2', Architectural Design vol. 63, nr. 3/4, march/april 1993, p. 91-93.

Richard, B., 'Robot Wars. Robotergestaltungen und -Phantasmen zwischen "Artificial Intelligence" und "Artificial Life"', Kunstforum nr. 130, Mai/Juli 1995, p. 190-211.

Scha, R., Vreedenburgh, E., 'Vers une autre Architecture', Zeezucht nr.8, september 1994, p. 6-14.

'Telecommunications', The Economist vol. 336, nr. 7934, september/october 1995, survey p. 5-40.

Virilio, P., 'The Law of Proximity', D: Columbia Documents of Architecture and Theory vol. two, 1993, Columbia University, New York, p. 123-137.

Symposium reports, exhibition catalogues:

Scha, R., Artificial, catalogus tentoonstelling, Amsterdam 1993.

Doors of Perception 2 Proceedings, 'Home', Netherlands Design Institute, Amsterdam november 1994.

Doors of Perception 3 Proceedings, 'Info-Eco Communities', Netherlands Design Institute, Amsterdam november 1995.

Levy, P., Welcome to Virtuality, Lezing Dutch Design Institute, Amsterdam 20 april 1995.

Multimediale 4, Zentrum für Kunst und Medientechnologie, Karlsruhe 1994.

Neonatuur, Stichting Phoenix en Theater Zeebelt, Den Haag september 1994.

COMPUTER AIDED DESIGN

Books:

Frazer, J., An Evolutionary Architecture, theme VII Architectural Association, London 1995.

Schmitt, G., Architectura et Machina. Computer Aided Architectural Design und Virtuelle Architektur, Vieweg & Sohn Verlagsgesellschaft, Braunschweig/Wiesbaden 1993.

Magazines - theme issues:

Arch+, Computerarchitektur, nr. 128, September 1995.

Articles:

Cooley, M., 'From Brunelleschi to CAD', World Architecture nr. 6, june 1990, p. 77-81.

Dijk, H. van, 'Vloeibare en geanimeerde barok. Het waterpaviljoen op de Neeltje Jans', Archis nr. 11, november 1995, p. 18-29.

Hotch, R., 'Matching Computers to Practice', Architecture nr. 6, june 1995, p. 141-143.

Koekebakker, O., 'Bouwen met bits, met de computer naar een Nieuwe Architectuur', Items nr. 7, 1995, p. 18-26.

McCullough, M., 'Designing Cities on Disk', Architecture nr. 4, april 1995,

p. 115-119.

Melet, E., 'De grenzen van het maakbare. Afvaloverstortplaats van Kas Oosterhuis', De Architect nr. 12, december 1995, p. 36-41.

Novotski, B.J., 'Gehry Forges New Computer Links', Architecture august 1992, p. 105-110.

Novotski, B.J., 'New Roles for Multimedia', Architecture may 1994, p. 165-167.

Novotski, B.J., 'Virtual Reality for Architects', Architecture october 1994, p. 121-125.

Oosterhuis, K., 'Gebouwen en steden zijn synthetische organismen', De Bouwadviseur december 1993, p. 46-50.

Oosterhuis, K., 'Artificiële intuïtie', De Architect nr. 57, Vertellingen, november 1995, p. 58-65.

Schmitt, G., e.a., Forschung und Entwicklung 94, ETH Zürich, Department Architektur, Zürich 1994.

Teicholz, E., Yu, L., 'The Promise of Multimedia', Progressive Architecture nr. 10, october 1993, p. 89-91.

Young, R., 'A Third Wave Practice', Progressive Architecture nr. 11, november 1992, p 106-108.

Yu, L., '3D Design: Cyberspace and Beyond', Progressive Architecture nr. 10, october 1991, p. 126-127.

INTELLIGENT BUILDINGS, SMART SPACES

Books:

Casciani, S., Dreams of Power. Reality and Utopia in Home Automation, BTicino/CittàStudiedizioni, Milano 1995.
Demil, C., Living Tomorrow. Het huis van de toekomst, Roularta Books VIF Editions, S.L. 1995.

Magazines - theme issues:

Arch+, Das Haus als Intelligente Haut, nr. 104, Juli 1990.
Arch+, Medienfassaden, nr. 108, August 1991.
Arch+, Wohltemperierte Architektur; Intelligente Planung, nr. 113, September 1992.

Articles:

Battle, G., McCarthy, C., 'Multi-Source Synthesis. A Future Engineering Response to Climatic Forces in Architecture', Architectural Design vol. 63, nr. 7/8, june/july 1993, p. 25-29.
Böhm, F., 'Glossar zur Solararchitektur', Arch+ nr. 126, April 1995, p. 68-73.
Krausse, J., 'The Other Half of Architecture', World Architecture nr. 25, 1993, p. 75-79.
MacInnes, K., 'Is Intelligent the Opposite

of Clever?', Architectural Design vol. 64, nr. 3/4, march/april 1994, p. X-XIII.
Spiller, N., 'When Is a Door a Door?', Architectural Design vol. 64, nr. 7/8, august 1994, p. XV-XIII.

VIRTUAL ARCHITECTURE AND URBANISM

Books:

Feireiss, K., Möller, C. (ed.) Christian Möller. Interaktive Architektur, (Book on the Occasion of Exhibition, Berlin 1994), Aedes und Autoren, Berlin 1994.
Lénárd, I., Oosterhuis, K., Rubens, M. (red.), Sculpture City. The Electronic Fusion between Architecture and Art, 010 Publishers, Rotterdam 1995.
Weibel, P., The Media Pavilion. Art and Architecture in the Age of Cyberspace, The Austrian Exhibition for the Biennale of Venice 1995, Springer Verlag, Wien 1995.

Magazines - theme issues:

Arch+, Vilém Flusser. Virtuelle Räume - Simultane Welten, nr. 111, März 1992.
Architectural Design, Architects in Cyberspace, vol. 65, nr. 11/12, november/december 1995.

Articles:

Craemer, S., 'Interactive Architecture', World Architecture nr. 39, 1995, p. 146-151.
Diller, E., Scofidio, R., 'reVIEWING', D: Columbia Documents and Theory vol. one, 1992, Columbia University, New York, p. 29-51.
Franck, G., 'Raum, Zeit und Aufmerksamkeit. Zum Einfluß der Telematik auf Stadt und Umwelt', Bauwelt vol. 81, nr. 22, 1990, p. 1089-1102.
Gilbert, N., 'Condition Zero', World Architecture nr. 26, 1993, p. 78-81.
Gilbert, N., 'Information plus Vernacular equals the Future', World Architecture nr. 29, 1993, p. 66-71.
'Institute for electronic clothing/Stephen Perrella and Tony Wrong (arch.)', Architectural Design vol. 62, nr. 11/12, november/december profile nr. 100 1992, p. 63-66.
Ito, T., 'Ein Garten der Mikrochips', Arch+ nr. 123, September 1994, p. 42-49.
Jacobs, K., 'Interface. Waiting for the Millennium part II', Metropolis july/august 1994, p. 49-53, p. 67-69.
Jacobs, K., 'Dinosauring the Future. Waiting for the Millennium: part III', Metropolis october 1994, p. 87-97.
Jacobs, K., 'In a World Built on Simulation, Your Dreams Can Come True. Waiting for the Millennium: Part IV', Metropolis january/february 1995, p. 55-

59, p. 85-87, p. 106.
Jacobs, K., 'On Line. An Ongoing Serie about Public, Private, and Electronic Space in America's Cities', Metropolis june 1995, p. 57-61, p. 80-85.
Jacobs, K., 'The City of the Future. An Ongoing Serie about Public, Private, and Electronic Space in America's Cities', Metropolis october 1995, p. 112-117, p. 149-159.
Jacobs, K., 'A Real City in a Virtual World.' Metropolis november 1995, p. 60-67, p. 69-75.
Krewani, A., Thomsen, C.W., 'Virtuelle Realitäten (Virtual Realities)', Daidalos nr. 41, september 1991, p. 118-119.
Kurgan, L., 'You are here Information Drift', assemblage nr. 25, december 1994, p. 17-43.
Lynn, G., 'Stranded Sears Tower', Architectural Design vol. 63, nr. 3/4, march/april profile nr.102 1993, p. 82-84.
Lynn, G., 'Multiplicitous and In-Organic Bodies', Architectural Design vol. 63, nr. 11/12, november/december profile 106 1993, p. 30-37.
Lynn, G., 'Leicht und Schwer', Arch+ nr. 124/125, December 1994, p. 38-43.
Mitchell, W.J., 'Electronic Urbanism: Bricks versus Bits?', Canadian Architect july 1995, p. 24-26.
Rötzer, F., 'Raum und Virtualität. Einige Anmerkungen', Kunstforum Bd. 121, 1993, p. 56-62.
Salat, S., Labbe, F., 'Architecture of the Virtual', World Architecture nr. 7, 1990, p. 74-77.
Salat, S., Labbe, F., Interviewed by Radian Gyurov; 'Transforming the Reality into an Architectural Image', World Architecture nr. 7, 1990, p. 78-85.
Sassen, S., 'Analytic Borderlands: Economy and Culture in the Global City', D: Columbia Documents of Architecture and Theory vol. three, 1993, Columbia University, New York, p. 5-23.

VIRTUAL ART

Books:

Hoogh, H. de, Bree, M. van, Brouwer, J. (ed.), DEAF95 Interfacing Realities, Catalogus Festival DEAF95, V2 Organisatie, Rotterdam 1995.
V2, Adriaansens, A. (ed.), Book for Unstable Media, 's-Hertogenbosch 1992.

Articles:

Holzer, J., 'Virtual Reality: an Emerging Medium', Art & Design vol. 9, nr. 11/12, november/december 1994, p. 9-15.
Pijnappel, J., 'Peter Weibel. Ars Electronica, an Interview', Art & Design vol. 9, nr. 11/12, november/december 1994, p. 26-31.
Pijnappel, J., 'Toshio Iwai. From the Flip-Book to the Museum in the Air, an Interview', Art & Design vol. 9, nr. 11/12,

november/december 1994, p. 89-93.
Rötzer, F., 'Neue Medien Diskussion. Neue Medien: WAS etwas ist - WIE etwas erscheint?', Kunstforum Bd. 122, 1993, p. 334-345.
Sawagari, N., 'Kodai Nakahara. Animate Home Electronics', Art & Design vol. 9, nr. 11/12,november/december 1994, p. 53-55.
Tisher, S., 'Virtuelle Gartenkunst in Videoclips / Virtual Garden Art in Videoclips', Topos nr. 11,Juni 1995, p. 132-140.

COLOFON

Biographical Details

Ole Bouman is a cultural historian. He is a writer, exhibition curator, film maker and consultant in the fields of architecture, visual culture and politics. He is an editor of Archis (an architectural monthly) and teaches at the Amsterdam School of the Arts. He co-authored The Invisible in Architecture, a far-ranging investigation into the cultural conditions prevailing in contemporary architecture. Bouman edited "And justice for all...", Maastricht 1994, a book about politics and visual culture. In 1995 he published two futuristic scenarios for Rotterdam 2045. He contributes regularly to international magazines and is currently organizing the Anyhow conference due to be held in Rotterdam in 1997.

Ben van Berkel studied architecture at the Gerrit Rietveld Academy in Amsterdam and the Architectural Association in London where he graduated in 1987. In 1988 he set up his own architectural practice together with Caroline Bos. Current projects include a new museum in Nijmegen, various housing and multifunctional projects as well as the Erasmus bridge in Rotterdam. Van Berkel has taught at Columbia University, New York and is Diploma Unit Master at the Architectural Association in London. Major publications:
- Mobile Forces, monograph, Ernst &
Sohn, Berlin 1994
- 'Ben van Berkel and Caroline Bos', monograph issue of A + U, Tokyo (May) 1995
- 'Ben van Berkel', monograph issue of El Croquis, Madrid (May) 1995.

Art director René van Raalte is a partner in BRS Premsela Vonk, designers and architects, where he is responsible for spatial design in the field of communications. He studied at the Gerrit Rietveld Academy in Amsterdam. His graphic and architectural work has included commissions for the PTT, Museon, The Ministry of Justice, the Ministry of Education and the Dutch Parliament.

RealSpace in QuickTimes
Architecture and Digitization

curator:
Ole Bouman
commissioner:
Rudolph Brouwers, Netherlands Architecture Institute, Rotterdam
architectural design:
Van Berkel en Bos Architectuurbureau bv, Amsterdam
Ben van Berkel (project architect)
Caspar Smeets (project coordinator)
Rob Hootsmans
Caroline Bos
Remco Bruggink
Freek Loos
Ger Gijzen
structural engineering:
Ingenieursbureau Zonneveld, b.v., Rotterdam
Jan van der Windt
Roel van der Bolt
Cock Molengraaf
Rijn van den Heuvel
art direction:
BRS Premsela Vonk, Amsterdam
René van Raalte
Paulette Peeters
Harold Houdijk
Michel Lotze
computergraphics, 3-D modelling:
Cees van Giessen
technical realization:
Vandie Interieurbouw, Maarssen
Frits Diepgrond
NAi staff involved
Just Schimmelpenninck
Martine van Nieuwenhuyzen
Anne Hoogewoning
Claire Beke
Lily Hermans
Jaqueline Engel
Astrid Karbaat

Sponsors:
Ingenieursbureau Zonneveld b.v., Rotterdam

Hollandsche Beton Maatschappij bv;

Hollandsche Beton en Waterbouw bv, Gouda

Drukkerij Rosbeek bv, Nuth

Boekbinderij Spiegelenberg, Zoetermeer

Centrum Hout, Almere

SYST-O-MATIC, een divisie van Nederland Haarlem, Haarlem

SYST·O·MATIC
EEN DIVISIE VAN NEDERLAND-HAARLEM

Co-Sponsors:
Hout- en Meubileringscollege, Amsterdam/Rotterdam
Rients Dijkstra, Amsterdam
Flame Guard, Nijmegen
Ingenieursbureau Grabowsky & Poort BV, Den Haag: Henk Dickhoff
This entry to the Triennale di Milano has been produced by the Netherlands Architecture Institute, at the invitation of the Netherlands Ministry of Education, Culture and Science, in collaboration with the Mondriaan Foundation and the Netherlands Fund for Architecture.

Film materials have been provided by:
Alias / Wavefront, Mountain View, USA
Van Berkel & Bos Architectuurbureau, Amsterdam, The Netherlands
BRTN, Brussels, Belgium
Instituut Calibre, Eindhoven, The Netherlands
Delft University of Technology / SIMONA, Delft, The Netherlands
Monika Fleischmann, Sankt Augustin, Germany
Cees van Giessen, Amsterdam, The Netherlands
Gira, Radeformwald, Germany
Agnes Hegedüs, Germany
Hollandse Signaal Apparaten, Hengelo, The Netherlands
IE Keyprocessor, Utrecht, The Netherlands
Invenit, Domotica Platform Nederland, Amsterdam, The Netherlands
IVS, Hoogwoud, The Netherlands
Montevideo / TBA, Netherlands Media Art Institute, Amsterdam, The Netherlands
Nemetschek Nederland bv, Leiden, The Netherlands
NOX Architecten, Rotterdam, The Netherlands
Kas Oosterhuis, Rotterdam, The Netherlands
Jan van de Pavert, Utrecht, The Netherlands
Philips Corporate Design, Eindhoven, The Netherlands
PTT Telecom, Groningen, The Netherlands
Paul Sermon, Leipzig, Germany
Jeffrey Shaw, Karlsruhe, Germany
Siemens Nederland, The Hague, The Netherlands
Stacey Spiegel, Los Angeles, USA
Staefa Control Systems, Zürich, Switzerland
TNO, Delft, The Netherlands
Universität Hamburg/Institut für Mathematik und Datenverarbeitung in der Medizin, Hamburg, Germany
Martijn Velthoen, Amsterdam, The Netherlands
Villa bv, Rotterdam, The Netherlands
Zentrum für Kunst und Medientechnologie, Karlsruhe, Germany
Zwarts & Jansma, Abcoude, The Netherlands

Publication:
This book is published in the context of the Dutch contribution to the XIX Milan Triennale, 28 February to 10 May 1996; 10 August to 17 November in the Netherlands Architecture Institute, Rotterdam.

This publication is partly based on articles in the magazine Archis.

Design:
BRS Premsela Vonk
René van Raalte
Frank van de Oudeweetering
van GOG ontwerpers, Amsterdam

Printing:
Drukkerij Rosbeek bv, Nuth

Book binding:
Boekbinderij Spiegelenberg, Zoetermeer

Production CD-Rom:
Harold Houdijk
Michel Lotze

Sound expo & CD-Rom:
Boris Nieuwenhuijzen
Hannah Bosma

Translation:
Robyn de Jong-Dalziel

Associate editing:
Jacqueline Engel
Astrid Karbaat

Production:
Astrid Vorstermans

Publisher:
Simon Franke

Credits illustrations:
P 4, 14, 16-19: Pavilion Milan Triennale,
courtesy Van Berkel & Bos
Architectuurbureau, Amsterdam
P 14: Still from Soft City, courtesy NOX
Architecten, Rotterdam
P 14: Still from Sculpture City, courtesy
Kas Oosterhuis, Rotterdam
P 17: Ingenieursbureau Zonneveld b.v.
P 18, 19: courtesy Cees van Giessen
P 29: Charles Cockerell, The Professor's
Dream, courtesy The Royal Academy of
Arts, London.
P 29: courtesy Fast Electronic GmbH,
München
P 37: digital city model of inner city
Berlin, courtesy Art + Com.
P 45: courtesy Raadgevend
Ingenieursbureau Beekink bv, Boskoop.

It was not possible to find all the
copyright holders of the illustrations
used. Interested parties are requested to
contact NAi Publishers, P.O. Box 237,
3000 AE Rotterdam, The Netherlands.

Available in North, South and Central
America through D.A.P./Distributed Art
Publishers 636 Broadway, 12th floor,
New York, NY 10012, Tel. 212 473-
5119 Fax 212 673-2887

Printed and Bound in The Netherlands